GAMES

FOR PEOPLE WITH
SENSORY IMPAIRMENTS

Strategies for Including Individuals of All Ages

Lauren J. Lieberman, PhD
SUNY Brockport

Jim F. Cowart,
California School for th

D0957640

Human Kinetics

Library of Congress Cataloging-in-Publication Data

Lieberman, Lauren J., 1965-
    Games for people with sensory impairments : strategies for
including individuals of all ages / Lauren J. Lieberman, Jim F.
Cowart.
      p.   cm.
    Includes bibliographical references.
    ISBN 0-87322-890-1
    1. Physical education for the blind.   2. Blind--Recreation.
3. Blind-deaf--Recreation.   4. Deaf--Recreation.   5. Physical
education for handicapped persons.   6. Handicapped--Recreation.
7. Games.   I. Cowart, Jim F., 1937-   . II. Title.
HV1767.L54   1996
371.91'13--dc20   96-2010
                                                  CIP

ISBN: 0-87322-890-1

Acquisitions Editor: Scott Wikgren; **Developmental Editor:** Elaine Mustain; **Assistant Editors:** Susan Moore-Kruse, Kent Reel, and Erin Cler; **Editorial Assistant:** Amy Carnes; **Copyeditor:** Regina Wells; **Proofreader:** Erin Cler; **Graphic Artist:** Julie Overholt; **Graphic Designer:** Stuart Cartwright; **Photo Editor:** Boyd LaFoon; **Cover Designer:** Jack Davis; **Photographers:** Kelly Butterworth, Monica Lepore, Monica Kleeman, Jim Cowart, Sue Fleming, and John Schrock; **Illustrator:** Studio 2-D; **Printer:** Versa Press

Human Kinetics books are available at special discounts for bulk purchase. Special editions or book excerpts can also be created to specification. For details, contact the Special Sales Manager at Human Kinetics.

Printed in the United States of America   10 9 8 7 6 5

Human Kinetics
Web site: www.HumanKinetics.com

United States: Human Kinetics, P.O. Box 5076, Champaign, IL 61825-5076
800-747-4457
e-mail: humank@hkusa.com

Canada: Human Kinetics, 475 Devonshire Road, Unit 100, Windsor, ON N8Y 2L5
800-465-7301 (in Canada only)
e-mail: orders@hkcanada.com

Europe: Human Kinetics, 107 Bradford Road, Stanningley
Leeds LS28 6AT, United Kingdom
+44 (0) 113 255 5665
e-mail: hk@hkeurope.com

Australia: Human Kinetics, 57A Price Avenue, Lower Mitcham, South Australia 5062
08 8277 1555
e-mail: liahka@senet.com.au

New Zealand: Human Kinetics, P.O. Box 105-231, Auckland Central
09-523-3462
e-mail: hkp@ihug.co.nz

Contents

This book is dedicated to the children from Perkins School for the Blind, the California School for the Blind, Oregon State University's Special Physical and Motor Fitness Clinic, and the many other children in our lives who have taught us what works best for moving, learning, and growing.

Acknowledgments

The authors gratefully acknowledge the following people:

Ann Cowart for her patience and motivation; Julian Stein for writing the foreword and for his encouragement; Monica Lepore for her energy, super activities, editing, and never-ending guidance; and Monica Kleeman for her understanding, creativity, and wonderful support. We would like to thank our wonderful photographers: Monica Lepore, Monica Kleeman, Kelly Butterworth, Jim Cowart, Sue Fleming, and John Schrock. We thank all the innovators because without their terrific input this book would not exist.

Lauren would like to thank her family for their support and understanding through the process; Carol Erickson for her encouragement; and Lou Lieberman for all his wonderful wisdom and belief through the years.

Foreword

Physical education teachers and activity leaders in the trenches are always on the lookout for appropriate, appealing games and activities for their students. Lauren Lieberman and Jim Cowart supply these resources through the pages of this practical, relevant, and realistic book, *Games for People With Sensory Impairments*. Drawing on their extensive experiences in teaching and reaching students of all ages who are blind, deaf and blind, or multihandicapped, the authors have assembled fitness, recreation, and aquatic activities for elementary through high school youths. There is something for everyone in this excellent publication. The principles they present for adapting games, activities, and procedures introduced as instructional strategies can be applied to situations involving nondisabled youngsters as well as those with disabilities. In fact, many of the activities you will read about can be used for students of all ages and levels of ability, without further adaptation.

The major focus of *Games for People With Sensory Impairments*, however, is on individuals who are blind, deaf and blind, or multihandicapped. Lieberman and Cowart carefully and clearly present methods and techniques to assist teachers and leaders in becoming more effective with their students or clients. Experienced teachers and leaders will find this publication an excellent resource of tried-and-true activities and approaches. Regardless of the length and type of experience readers possess, they will find new ideas that will result in higher quality programs for their students.

For novices, this publication provides a wealth of information on what to do, how to do it, and why. This valuable resource should stimulate readers' creativity, resourcefulness, and initiative to explore further and develop additional games and activities for their students.

The games and activities included are, for the most part, creative innovations by outstanding teachers and leaders in special schools or programs for students who have sensory impairments. These games, however, are adaptations of familiar activities found in virtually every good physical-education or motor-development curriculum. It is apparent that even for students who are blind, multihandicapped, or deaf and blind, no special curriculum and few, if any, specific activities exist only for them. Activities for these students are basically the same activities that have attracted students since time immemorial.

Even though implications of these activities are for segregated programs or special classes, the actual content and easily accomplished, common-sense adaptations and accommodations make their application appropriate for integrated and mainstreamed classes. These activities are educational and have both general goals and specific objectives. The authors, however, aware that learning is accomplished most effectively in environments of enjoyment, pleasure, and fun, focus on the learner and learning (not the teacher and teaching). Success in any learning-teaching situation is best when teachers and leaders know their stuff, know who they are stuffing, and then stuff them wisely! These important underlying principles are demonstrated throughout the pages of this excellent book. Heartiest congratulations to the authors on an outstanding professional job, for which we all say, "Thanks for sharing your experiences and expertise with us—and well done."

Julian U. Stein
Professor in Physical Education (Retired)
George Mason University
Fairfax, Virginia

About the Innovators

Karen Allen has been teaching at the Oklahoma School for the Blind since 1979. She teaches students who are visually impaired with multiple disabilities and is on the Oklahoma Special Olympics Program Committee. For this committee she works on adapting sports and creates programs for teaching kindergarten and third through fifth grades.

Jim Cowart has taught all ranges of abilities throughout his 33 1/2 years of teaching. He is currently at the California School for the Blind in Fremont, California. He has contributed to many journals in the area of adapted physical education relating to teaching and adapting equipment. Jim is the 1995 Adapted Physical Education Teacher of the Year for the Southwest Alliance for Health, Physical Education, Recreation and Dance, and the National Adapted Physical Education Teacher of the Year for AAHPERD. (More information about Jim can be found in the About the Authors section on page 145.)

Sue Fleming has taught regular physical education in both junior high and elementary school in Sitka, Alaska for the past 25 years. She currently teaches kindergarten and third, fourth, and fifth grades. She is proficient at adapting games to meet the needs of her students with visual impairments.

Linda Gingery has retired after 25 years of teaching at the Michigan School for the Blind in East Lansing, Michigan. Linda's energy and enthusiasm were an inspiration to all her students.

Formerly on the staff at Gaenslin Orthopedic School in Milwaukee, Wisconsin, **Sue Grosse** teaches physical education at the Milwaukee High School of the Arts. She is also an Adapted Aquatics Instructor Trainer for the American Red Cross and has edited several Practical Pointer Manuals through the American Alliance for Health, Physical Education, Recreation and Dance.

Beth Hudy currently teaches physical education and swimming at the Royer Greaves School for the Blind in Paoli, Pennsylvania. She teaches students who are blind and students who are visually impaired with multiple disabilities. She is also a volleyball coach at West Chester University in West Chester, Pennsylvania.

Stephen Kearney has been teaching at the Oklahoma School for the Blind for over 20 years. He teaches K–12 and also coaches goal ball. He has coached teams from all over the world, including the World Cup team for three years in a row. He is also very active in The United States Association for Blind Athletes.

Monica Kleeman has taught at the Perkins School for the Blind in Watertown, Massachusetts for the past five years in the Deaf/Blind Program, Life Skills, and Adult Services. Monica also coaches the swim team, track team, and goal ball team at Perkins and is an expert in adapted aquatics. She is also a recreation director for the Lowell Association for the Blind in Lowell, Massachusetts.

Monica Lepore has taught for 13 years at West Chester University in West Chester, Pennsylvania preparing physical educators for including students with disabilities in physical activity programs. She has a doctorate in leadership in adapted physical education from New York University. She has taught swimming at the Light House for the Blind, United Cerebral Palsy, and various Red Cross community programs.

Lauren Lieberman taught at the Perkins School for the Blind for five years in the Life Skills, Head Injury, and Deaf/Blind Program. Lauren also coached goal ball and track. In 1995 she received her doctorate from Oregon State University in Corvallis, Oregon in movement studies for the disabled. She now teaches at the State University of New York at Brockport. (More information about Lauren can be found in the About the Authors section on page 145.)

Eric Patterson has been teaching physical education and aquatics at the Oregon School for the Blind in Salem, Oregon for the past five years. He teaches students who are blind, visually impaired with multiple disabilities, and deaf-blind. Eric is also a volunteer coach for the Oregon Games for the Physically Limited, and the Oregon Special Olympics.

Candice Rehmeier has 17 years of teaching experience in all levels of education, including special populations in the area of physical education. Honors include the Cooper Foundation Excellence in Teaching Award and being named a Christa McAuliffe Prize Honoree. She is currently teaching at the Nebraska School for the Visually Handicapped in Nebraska City, Nebraska.

John Schrock has been teaching at the Missouri School for the Blind for more than 18 years. He also coaches track and swimming. John is the National Chairman for powerlifting for the United States Association for Blind Athletes, and was the team leader for two World Cup Powerlifting Championships.

Doug Smith has taught regular physical education for nine years. He holds an endorsement in adapted physical education. He has taught at the Philip

J. Rock Center and School for Individuals Who Are Blind and Visually Impaired for over 10 years. Mr. Smith continues to take courses to assist with ongoing programs at his school.

Linda Webbert taught physical education at the Maryland School for the Blind in Baltimore, Maryland. She has been president of the Eastern Athletic Association of the Blind and has served on the board of directors for the Maryland Special Olympics.

Preface

This manual is designed for adapted physical education specialists, physical education teachers, classroom teachers, therapeutic recreation specialists, community recreation leaders, and parents. It is specifically geared to those who—in segregated or inclusive settings—are responsible for students and/or adults who are sensory impaired or who are sensory impaired with multiple disabilities. By sensory impaired with multiple disabilities we mean having one or more disabilities in addition to visual or hearing impairment. For example, a person may be mentally retarded and blind, orthopedically impaired and blind, deaf-blind, or cerebral palsied and blind. This book was also developed to meet the needs of sensory impaired students without disabilities, students with disabilities who are neither blind nor deaf, and adults with disabilities who are no longer in a formal educational setting.

Teachers and specialists working with students who are sensory impaired with multiple disabilities face unique challenges. Because such students make up a small percentage of the population, physical education texts on adaptations, instructional strategies, and activities for groups give only minimal information about working with them. Even less resource material is available about adults with disabilities who have progressed beyond the educational system. The daily challenges and frustrations resulting from this lack of information motivated us to write this book.

To produce a useful book we solicited physical education teachers from across the country who were teaching students with sensory impairments and multiple disabilities to contribute two or three of their best activities. Then we selected from among activities and games that reinforce skills, stress movement, and emphasize inclusion. All of these activities have been proven successful in both school and recreational settings. Every photo in this book includes children or adults who are sensory impaired, and illustrate that these activities are fun for all age and ability groups.

The activities offered in this book can all be presented to students who are sensory impaired with multiple disabilities within a regular physical education curriculum or to adults with sensory impairments in any recreational setting. But because these students and adults have unique combinations of impairments, modification is often required to ensure successful participation. Part I focuses on program adaptations and instructional strategies for successful participation. Common adaptations are listed under each activity; however, since even these may not be sufficient to meet the needs of all students or clients, the suggestions presented in "Adapting Games and Activities" will provide additional guidelines for making necessary adaptations.

Students in a regular physical education program typically learn skills through observation and practice. Many students who are visually impaired with multiple disabilities need to be taught movement skills in different ways, however, in order to succeed. For this reason, we have included a range of instructional techniques that have been successfully used to teach such students. The method you choose will depend on the sensory abilities of the individual, with the goal of maximizing student-teacher communication. You will find practical instructional strategies reviewed in here, with examples of their use.

Part II includes activities offered by physical education teachers experienced in working with students who are sensory impaired with multiple disabilities. The groups that appear at the top of the Game Finder will help you find games that meet your teaching or recreational needs; the Game Finder includes category, sport skills, physical and motor fitness, and fundamental motor patterns and skills.

If you work with young adults with multiple disabilities, you will find that many of the activities in *Games for People With Sensory Impairments* are appropriate for your clients. The need for fun through physical activity doesn't stop when a person leaves school. The activities we've included in the recreation category specifically address this need. Additionally, many of the games in the high school category may also be used with these young adults.

Our goal in education is to help every student develop his or her full potential. We believe that if we deal positively and creatively with the challenges presented by students who are sensory impaired with multiple disabilities, these children, too, can develop physically, emotionally, and intellectually through the fun of games and exercise. Our hope in working with adults with disabilities is to provide them with opportunities for whatever physical activity experiences they might desire or benefit from. One way to do this is to become more knowledgeable in teaching strategies, program adaptations, and activities geared specifically for these students and adults. In this manual we have expanded our own knowledge, and we hope it will expand your resources and knowledge as well.

How to Use This Book

Teachers and specialists often use games, both to help students develop and refine their movement skills and to engage adults in enjoyable physical activity that produces health benefits. For the students and adults alike, these games can provide enjoyable experiences. For efficient learning to take place within a game, however, or for adults to participate successfully and enjoyably, the game leader must provide sound thought, careful planning, and suitable instruction.

By following the four steps given here, you can use this book most effectively to develop your use of games with students and adults. Note that although the steps are written with a school setting in mind, they will usually be applicable also in settings with adults with disabilities.

Step 1—Locate an age-appropriate game that meets the needs of all students within the class.

Use the Game Finder to locate an age-appropriate game, being aware of the skills to emphasize with each student in the class. For example, an elementary physical education teacher has a class of 30 pupils who are ages seven and eight, among them Sam, who is hemiplegic and visually impaired. Objectives for the students in the class focus on basic movement patterns (the objective in Sam's Individual Education Plan focuses on the development of locomotor patterns). The instructor wants to identify games that stress the movement patterns. She follows the steps suggested in the Game Finder to locate a game that seems to meet the movement needs of her student Sam. She sees that the game Bright Objects, for example, emphasizes basic movement patterns. She repeats this process to identify additional appropriate games for the class.

Step 2—Examine the game to confirm its suitability for students; make only needed modifications.

Once a game is located, the instructor determines if it can be played in the school's facility, if the necessary supplies are available, if the game's rules and strategies are within the students' mental capacities, and if students have the necessary social and game skills to participate. In this case, the teacher believes the game Bright Objects can be played in the school's multipurpose room, which has sufficient beanbags and other items to be used; the students have demonstrated the mental and social skills needed to play the game; and the children will be utilizing various locomotor skills (such as hopping, galloping, and skipping) they have recently learned and practiced. Sam's vision and locomotor skills allow him to differentiate most colors and shapes, and he walks and performs a modified run. Following this review of the game, the instructor believes no specific adaptations for Sam or any other student need be made. If a game or skill modification were necessary, the instructor would refer to the points listed under "Specific Considerations" in Part I.

Step 3—Implement and monitor the game's effectiveness.

Having satisfactorily completed the analysis in Step 2, the instructor introduces the game to the class. This brings into play one of the more critical elements of teaching, namely, monitoring student progress during game play. The instructor keeps the game moving smoothly by implementing game rules, by giving positive reinforcement when warranted, and by making any necessary corrections. If challenges arise during the game, the instructor makes needed adjustments in the game or play skills to keep the students actively involved in skill development. This may entail challenging some pupils more and other pupils less. The "Adapting Games and Activities" section of this book provides useful suggestions for modifications. For problems that do not require immediate solutions, an instructor should make a mental note for consideration before the game is played again.

Step 4—Reexamine the game's appropriateness.

At this point the instructor may simply confirm that the choice of the game was good—it allowed students to practice needed skills or develop new ones in an enjoyable way. On the other hand, this could be a time to decide that the game, as presented, was inappropriate for the students. If the instructor felt students were not challenged, the game could be modified or new skills taught—the game could be made more difficult to encourage student growth. If the students were not successful, the instructor might consider changing the game to lessen the challenge or might select a different game that presents a more appropriate challenge for students. Whatever the decision, the "Specific Considerations" section in Part I can provide very useful information for making successful changes. Sam, for example, was able to walk and perform a modified run, and he could identify and retrieve objects of various colors and sizes. The instructor chose to challenge Sam further by teaching him to hop on his noninvolved foot. Teaching techniques covered in "Instructional Strategies" proved invaluable to the instructor for teaching Sam to hop.

Games for People With Sensory Impairments enables teachers and group leaders to implement these steps by providing an easy-to-follow Game Finder on page 27, guidelines for individualizing games, and instructional strategies for teaching game skills. These resources will help you include children who are visually impaired with multiple disabilities in enjoyable physical activities with nonhandicapped children, while challenging them all. These features will be equally useful in helping adults with disabilities enjoy successful participation in physical activity.

Part I

Adapting and Teaching Games and Activities

Adapting Games and Activities

Education is committed to the development of each student to the fullest extent possible. A number of curricular areas have been established to achieve this purpose, including physical education. Through the medium of movement, physical education contributes to the development of physical and motor fitness, fundamental movement skills and patterns, and skills in aquatics, dance, individual and group games, and sports.

Because many students with multiple disabilities cannot take advantage of unstructured participation in physical education, they often are not given the opportunity to develop skills within their ability, nor do they learn to play specific games or sports. With some creative thought and imagination, however, program adaptations can be made to accommodate these learners. Through adapted activities, students' skills may be improved, and they are enabled to learn and use new and specific game skills. In this way, education fulfills its responsibility of maximizing each student's opportunity to learn.

Every child deserves the maximum opportunity to learn.

GENERAL CONSIDERATIONS

The following strategies are important when considering activity adaptations for learners who are blind with multiple disabilities.

STUDENT ABILITIES

Good instructors assess the strengths and weaknesses of a student with a disability before involving that student in their movement programs. This analysis should include information regarding both the extent of visual impairment, hearing impairment, and any other health problems. Such knowledge can be obtained from classroom teachers, student health records, parents, physical therapists, and/or family physicians. With this information, the instructor will have a general idea of what activity adaptations may be needed to accommodate the student.

Present level of functioning and any needed adaptations can be confirmed by having the student demonstrate designated skills. A useful strategy for determining the current level of functioning of a student with a disability in relation to a non-disabled peer is to conduct a Discrepancy Analysis (Brown, Shiraga, York, Zanella, and Rogan, 1984). By comparing a child with a disability to a child without, differences can be identified and analyzed, and appropriate adaptations can be made.

SPECIFIC ACTIVITIES

Activities offered in adapted physical education should show little difference from those offered in regular physical education. It is important for instructors to know all aspects of activities (i.e., equipment, rules, skills, etc.). In addition, it is critical for the teacher to have the knowledge and ability to task-analyze skills (i.e., the ability to break a skill down into its component parts for learning purposes). This expertise enables teachers to make necessary modifications to accomodate students while making sure that activities maintain their basic intent or original character.

AGE-APPROPRIATE ACTIVITIES

Program emphasis should be on assisting students to acquire skills functionally appropriate for their age, and activities that encourage interaction with non-disabled peers. If you do not understand what is age-appropriate, look at the curriculum of a good regular physical education program with children of the same age as your students. As noted earlier, though many learners who are sensory impaired with multiple disabilities cannot participate unrestricted in activities with their classmates, through activity adaptation it is possible to help them both develop useful skills appropriate for their age and interact with peers.

SPECIFIC CONSIDERATIONS

It may be necessary to make changes in any or all of the areas noted below in order to accommodate these special learners in activities.

RULE MODIFICATION

By changing a rule or rules, an activity can be made less complex or restrictive in order to include students who are sensory impaired with multiple disabilities. Rules can be categorized as rules related to play or rules related to players.

Play Rules

Play rules are rules that govern game play. Below are some examples of adaptations of these rules:

- A batter in softball is out when a fielder stops a rolling audible ball or when the fielders perform some type of cooperative drill before the runner reaches the base. For example, after fielding the ball, the defending team might be required to form a line and pass the ball from one end to the other, alternating over the head and between the legs.

- A runner in softball or kickball is awarded a point for reaching first base safely.

- A wheelchair tennis player is permitted to let the ball bounce two or three times (if needed) before playing the ball.

- A player in shuffleboard earns point values of 3, 2, and 1 instead of 10, 8, and 7 due to cognitive needs.

- A student is allowed to dribble a basketball by bouncing and catching the ball.

In order to achieve an out, the fielding team tries to complete this cooperative game before the runner reaches the base.

Player Rules

Successful participation in activities may require adjustment in player position, teaming of players, number of players, etc. Noted below are some examples of rule modifications related to players:

- Two players are in touch with each other in a game like "squat tag" (i.e., elbow to elbow, back to back, etc).

- A sighted guide runs with the base runner in a kickball or softball game.

- A student limited in movement plays only the defensive position in soccer.

- Additional players are included in Goal Ball to more adequately cover the playing area.

- A sighted person assists a blind participant in golf putting by pointing out ball location, distance of ball from the cup, and so on.

EQUIPMENT AND/OR FACILITIES MODIFICATION

Few major equipment and/or facility adaptations are necessary in low-level organized activities for most learners who are sensory impaired with or

A student uses a ball on a string to practice kicking. In this way, she gets automatic feedback on each kick and does not have to chase the ball.

without multiple disabilities; however, more specific or more complex adaptations may be needed in team, dual, or individual sports. Consider the benefit of adapting equipment or facilities that would have previously eliminated a student who is visually impaired with multiple disabilities from participating. Following are examples of equipment and facilities modified to encourage the learner in movement activities:

- Using an audible ball or anything else as a directional cue or goal in a tag game such as Steal the Bacon.
- Defining the playing area with mats, walls, cord with tape over it, and the like for any game that requires a defined playing area.
- Employing a rail for guidance in the approach in bowling.
- Using a bell, a portable radio, hand clapping, and so forth as a directional cue in relays (each team uses a different sound).
- Attaching a beeper to a stake or arch for auditory tracking in croquet.
- Using a short-handled putter in golf for a student in a wheelchair.

- Using a tug-of-war rope on the ground as a boundary for games such as volleyball.

SKILL MODIFICATION

Within a class including students who are sensory impaired with multiple disabilities, teachers will likely have a tremendous range of student abilities. By knowing where participants stand in the continuum of acquired skills, teachers can make adjustments that allow each learner to use and refine a skill or skills within his or her repertoire while enjoying active game participation. Some examples of skill adjustments to capitalize on each learner's present level of functioning follow:

- In tag games, each student uses fundamental motor patterns within his or her skill repertoire.
- In T-ball, a student with crutches uses one of his or her crutches as a bat.
- In bowling, a pupil uses a one-, two-, four-, or five-step delivery, depending on the individual's capabilities.
- In swimming, a student with spastic cerebral palsy uses a "toes-in" bilateral leg kick when performing an elementary backstroke.
- In bowling, horseshoes, and golf putting, a student who is very involved with cerebral palsy with limited head control uses a mercury switch to activate game equipment.

INSTRUCTIONAL MODIFICATIONS: MOVEMENT EXPLORATION

This teaching technique is a method of teaching movement skills that uses problem solving. It does not emphasize one "correct" body movement or dynamic quality. Its unique advantage is that for a specific challenge or problem, a variety of acceptable responses can be made. No child's success is determined or affected by the performance of another learner. For students who are sensory impaired with multiple disabilities, the approach can allow for successful participation by a learner with other students no matter how limited the learner may be. For example, students without sight and with additional disabilities can respond to such challenging questions from the instructor as

- "Can you go across . . . ?",
- "Show me another way . . .",
- "How many different ways . . . ?",
- "See if you can go . . .", or
- "How can you move . . . ?"

The responsibility of the teacher when using an exploratory approach is to present a series of suitable challenges from simple to complex depending on each child's capabilities.   If this strategy is implemented appropriately, continued self improvement by each learner will take place.

CONCLUSION

Review the general and specific suggestions discussed previously when considering an activity adaptation. If you are unsure of how to proceed, study the examples of adaptations that are included. It is important for instructors to remember that the key consideration in making an adaptation or adapta-

Programs that make appropriate adaptations and set students up for success from the beginning enhance students' growth.

tions is the value to be derived by the student. More detailed information related to specific adaptations can be obtained from the resources noted on page 10, as well as in the game section of this manual (Part II).

REFERENCE

Brown, L., Shiraga, B., York, J., Zanella, K., and Rogan, P. (1984). "The Discrepancy Analysis Technique in Programs for Students With Severe Handicaps." Paper, University of Wisconsin-Madison.

SELECTED RESOURCES

Adams, R.C., Daniels, A.N., McCubbin, J.A., and Rullman, L. (1982). *Games, Sports and Exercises for the Physically Handicapped.* Philadelphia: Lea and Febiger.

Anderson, L., and Greaves, E. (1980). *101 Activities for Physically Handicapped Children.* Palo Alto, CA: Peek Publications.

Breen, J., and Cratty, B. (1972). *Educational Games for Physically Handicapped Children.* Denver: Love Publishing Co.

Catarazulo, M., and Lolli, D. (1982). "A Motor Activities Manual for the Multi-Impaired." Unpublished grant project. Perkins School for the Blind, Watertown, MA.

Croke, K., and Fairchild, B. (1978). *Let's Play Games.* Chicago: The National Easter Seals Society for Crippled Children and Adults.

Dell, S., and McNerney, P. (1992). "Art and Games: Sensational Experiences for Students With Deaf-Blindness." Unpublished grant project from The Rhode Island Services to Children With Deaf-Blindness.

Division of Recreation, Education Department and Transmanian State Schools Sports Council. (1983). *A Child Is Not a Little Adult: Modifying Approaches to Sport for Australian Children.* Obtained from North American Youth Sports Institute, Kernersville, NC.

French, R.W., and Jansma, P. (1982). *Special Physical Education.* Columbus, OH: Charles E. Merrill Publishing Co.

Grosse, S. (1989). *The Best of Practical Pointers.* Reston, VA: AAHPERD.

Grosse, S. (1991). *Sports Instruction for Individuals With Disabilities: The Best of Practical Pointers.* Reston, VA: AAHPERD.

Grosse, S., and Thompson, D. (1993). *Sports, Recreation, and Leisure for Individuals With Disabilities: The Best of Practical Pointers.* Reston, VA: AAHPERD.

Kelley, J. (ed.) (1981). *Recreation Programming for Visually Impaired Children and Youth.* New York: American Foundation for the Blind.

Kratz, L.E. (1973). *Movement Without Sight.* Palo Alto, CA: Peek Publications.

Marsallo, M., and Vacante, D. (1983). *Adapted Games and Developmental Motor Activities for Children.* Annandale, VA: Marsallo/Vacante, 4608 Exeter Street.

Morris, G.S.D. (1976). *How to Change the Games Children Play.* Minneapolis: Burgess Publishing Co.

Rickards, P. (1986). *Popular Activities and Games for Blind, Visually Impaired and Disabled People.* Victoria, Australia: Association for the Blind. Distributed by AFB.

Vodola, T. (1978). *Diagnostic-Prescriptive Motor Ability and Physical Fitness Tasks and Activities.* Neptune City, NJ: Vec.

Instructional Strategies

Typically, students gain information through sight and hearing. Other avenues by which individuals obtain information are through tactile (touch), kinesthetic (muscles, tendons, and joints), and vestibular (balance information from the inner ear) senses. When students with impairments such as mental retardation, hearing loss, and/or physical disabilities experience the added disability of vision loss, the remaining senses must be used to fill the void.

In order to obtain insight into a student's preferred means for gaining information, the instructor should talk with the student, classroom teacher, and/or parent, as well as refer to school and health records. Once channels

The student uses a harness and rope for support, and the instructor provides appropriate assistance to guide the student safely to success on a climbing wall.

more commonly used by the student are identified, and the intact senses for getting information have been determined, the teacher should try to match instructional strategies to the student. Brailling and physical guidance (both taken from Cowart, 1993), explanation, and demonstration may be used to broaden the pupils' learning. In this chapter, each of these four commonly used teaching strategies will be briefly reviewed. Pointers to think about when considering their use will also be discussed. Finally, to assist the reader in planning and applying these strategies, two examples will be presented: One example stresses teaching of a sport skill, while the other makes use of techniques to teach rules and strategies of the game.

BRAILLING

Fait (1978) defines *brailling* as inspection of people or objects with the hands. Vodola (1973) uses the word "see", and Reams (1980) "tactile

The student brailles the instructor in a warm-up activity.

exploration" to refer to the same thing. For purposes of this manual, the term *brailling* refers to the student using his or her tactile senses in learning.

Brailling is an effective method of helping the student who is blind or visually impaired with multiple disabilities understand and learn skills. When considering the use of brailling as a teaching technique, keep the following points in mind.

■ When brailling, the pupil examines with his or her hands the position of the demonstrator's body, limb(s), and/or movement of the body parts as the skill is demonstrated.

■ Brailling is of particular value when teaching a new skill or when making a correction in an awkward or improper movement of the student.

■ Brailling is sometimes more effective for skills in which the body is stationary and the limbs move (e.g., archery).

■ Some skills are difficult to braille if the pupil is required to follow two or more moving body parts at the same time (e.g., four-step delivery in bowling); in this case an alternate teaching technique, such as physical assistance with verbal or sign prompts, may need to be emphasized.

■ Careful analysis of the skill by the teacher prior to instruction will help determine if brailling will be a good technique to use.

■ An assistant may be needed to help the student assume the appropriate position and placement of his or her hands during the execution of the skill.

■ When done properly, brailling allows the student not only to know the location of the body and its parts during skill execution but to become aware of speed and rhythm as well.

PHYSICAL GUIDANCE

Physical guidance is defined by Sulzer-Azaroff and Mayer (1991) as the teaching technique of performing a movement with the student, who then eventually gets the feel of the motion. It consists of placing the student's body and/or limb(s)—with or without an implement—into the appropriate position and putting him or her through the desired movement at the preferred speed. As with brailling, physical guidance is a primary teaching technique for assisting some students who are visually impaired with multiple disabilities to learn new skills and/or to correct bad habits. If done properly, physical guidance can be extremely beneficial in communicating the proper performance of a skill.

The instructor provides the minimum physical assistance necessary.

Points proven helpful when planning and using physical guidance are:

■ Always keep in mind that the goal of instruction is for the student to perform the skill at the most independent level possible.

■ Physical guidance can range from physically assisting the pupil totally through a skill to a gentle touch aimed at prompting the student to complete a task.

■ Begin with the amount of assistance that will ensure the desired performance of the skill. Generally, by trial and error the instructor will get an indication of assistance needed for successful performance of the task. With complex skills such as golf putting, the amount of assistance may vary with each step of the putting sequence.

■ Always use verbalization or sign with physical guidance to maximize skill learning.

■ Be constantly alert to pupil response. When you feel the student begin to perform the movement pattern or step(s) in a skill sequence, minimize your assistance accordingly. Try to phase out assistance as soon as possible to prevent student dependence.

■ Immediately reinforce the successful completion of a task or skill sequence. The intent is to increase the probability that the level of skill performance will occur again.

■ As with brailling, the position while providing assistance is critical. A proper assistance position does not interfere with the natural rhythm of the movement as the instructor feels the student begin to perform the task. (The position the instructor takes with a smaller student may not be the same with a larger student.)

■ When possible, have the student practice the skill under the conditions in which it will be used, reducing the necessity for later adjustments.

■ If a student resists being physically assisted, do not attempt to force performance of the skill. Allow the pupil to calm down, and then try again. If the student continues to resist physical guidance, reevaluate what is being done. The teacher may need to set up a behavior management program, teach another skill, or reposition him or herself for providing assistance.

EXPLANATION

In physical education, many pupils use their sense of hearing to gain information about skill development and game rules and strategy. However, auditory learning may be difficult or impossible for some of the pupils. In these instances, sign or body language may be used to communicate. Considering the following points may influence your success with this teaching strategy.

■ To assist individuals who are hearing-impaired and blind in making full usage of their remaining hearing, the instructor must seek information about the loss, conditions under which hearing is best, and other communication abilities and skills. As noted earlier, this information may be obtained from school staff, parents, records, or personal observation.

■ After becoming familiar with the student's mental capabilities, use whichever language (oral or sign) is appropriate for the pupil's functioning level to portray key points of the skill.

1. For more involved students with usable hearing, choose a few action words that focus on the desired skill or parts of the skill. If the student lacks hearing but has some usable vision, develop a sign or body movement that can create the correct image of the desired skill or its parts. In the case of a pupil who has no hearing or sight, the solution may be to manually move the student's hands through the sign(s) or movement pattern(s).

2. More highly functioning students can be given a more thorough explanation of the skill, providing a more complete picture of what is requested or what is to follow. The information should be presented in the sequence in which it will be performed.

■ When possible, combine verbal (sign) communication with brailling, physical guidance, or demonstration to increase learning efficiency.

■ Following the explanation, observe the student's response in order to check his or her understanding of how the skill is to be performed. If the pupil seems to be having difficulty comprehending the instructions, try the following:

1. Repeat the instructions, along with any related teaching strategy.

2. Search for another word, sign, gesture, or movement to communicate the desired skill.

■ Initial progress may be slow for some students with dual sensory impairments because they may be having to associate language with the movement at the same time they are trying to learn the desired skill. Always associate language with the movement, whatever the level of the individual.

■ Once the student's skill response is somewhat established, gradually reduce or remove any of the more artificial verbal or sign prompts, keeping only a natural cue or cues that are typically used to initiate the desired movement or skill.

DEMONSTRATION

Learning through the use of sight can take several forms: demonstrations, pictures, illustrations, or film. According to Winnick (1990) this channel of learning is preferred by the majority of sighted people. Of the sources of visual information, demonstration is probably used most often in physical education. Demonstration can communicate how a skill should be executed, a game should be played, or a dance should be performed. In a well executed demonstration, the skill is performed with good form and the pupil follows with an attempt to imitate the movement. For many students who are visually impaired with multiple disabilities, of course, demonstration is impractical and must be replaced with brailling, physical guidance, and explanation.

When considering use of demonstration for a student with some residual vision, the following may be helpful:

The student responds positively to the instructor's demonstration.

■ The demonstrator should be able to efficiently perform the skill as it would normally be done. In this way the pupil will have an accurate image of the skill to model.

■ If possible, combine demonstration with an explanation (oral or sign) and/or physical guidance to maximize the student's learning.

■ If a student does have sight, it is important to determine the extent of his or her vision. Each student's visual capabilities are unique, and an individual's visual functioning may fluctuate from day to day and from one setting to another (Kelley, 1981). Knowing this will help the instructor decide if demonstration can be a useful teaching strategy for a particular student, and will help provide the best conditions in which to demonstrate.

■ Demonstration should be followed by a time for practice. If the student is having difficulty modeling the skill, consider the following:

1. Repeat the demonstration as well as any related teaching strategies. Make any adjustments appropriate to improve the student's chances of understanding how to perform the desired movement.

2. If necessary, break complex skills (shooting an arrow, bowling a ball, etc.) into sub-skills, or component parts; lead the student to learn each

part separately, using demonstration and related teaching strategies. Finally, encourage pupils to integrate the parts into complete skills, again using demonstrations as the models.

■ Instructors should reinforce modeled performance as well as give feedback (including additional demonstrations, if necessary) to correct performance errors. This approach is repeated until the desired level of mastery is achieved, or adjustment made to conform with the student's capabilities.

CASE STUDIES

Following are two examples of the use of instructional strategies. The first emphasizes use of physical guidance and manually moving the student's hands to communicate and assist the student to learn a swim stroke. The second example stresses application of demonstration, physical guidance, and signing to communicate and help a pupil understand how to play dodgeball.

EXAMPLE #1

Sport: Swimming

Skill: Swim stroke, prone

Background: The student is a 14-year-old boy who is totally deaf and blind with some spasticity in the lower limbs; his primary sources for information are assisted signing (manually moving his hands through the sign) and physical guidance. He has generally resisted learning new skills.

Initial Observations: The student has good breath control; he demonstrates no swim stroke; bobbing and spinning in the water are his preferred activities; he resists being placed prone or supine in the water.

Student Objective: To learn a useful stroke. A beginner stroke is selected for emphasis, starting with an alternating arm pattern, since the student has some lower-leg involvement.

Instructional Plan: Because of the student's resistance to learning new skills, a behavior modification approach to teaching the alternating arm pattern is selected. Potato chips are very strong reinforcers; the plan

is to have the classroom teacher on the pool deck with the reinforcers for the student.

The instructor and student are in the water several feet from the poolside, with the instructor positioned so that he can manually move the student's hands to communicate the desired activity, as well as give the physical guidance that the student will likely need to perform the skill. The instructor manually moves the student's hands through the sign "you swim." Then the instructor quickly puts the student into the prone position on his (the teacher's) thigh. While in this position, the teacher alternates the student's arms as he moves with the student to the poolside. On touching the poolside, the instructor lets the pupil stand and manually moves the student's hand through the sign "good swimming." The classroom teacher immediately reinforces the pupil with a chip.

Evaluation: The instruction took place as planned. The student initially resists the practice, but he enjoys receiving the chips. It is decided to continue the plan as noted above.

Continued Instruction: The chips are used because they are a strong stimulus for continued practice, but are decreased as the student exhibits less resistance. Within a short time, the pupil anticipates what the teacher is going to sign, and he immediately performs a bilateral arm pattern (modified breaststroke arm pattern). At this point, the instructor no longer emphasizes an alternate arm pattern and reduces the physical assistance to just supporting the student's hips. Additionally, performing the swim stroke now seems to be its own motivation for the student, so the use of chips is eliminated.

Gradually the student's arm strokes become stronger, and he begins breathing every few strokes; physical assistance is removed, and the student swims independently.

EXAMPLE #2

Activity: Dodgeball

Background: The student is a 10-year-old boy with some residual sight, no hearing, and who is highly distractable. He learns new skills through signing words, demonstration, and physical assistance. The student demonstrates good movement skills.

In addition, he recently has been attending to tasks for longer periods of time as a result of a behavior management program. Because of his good physical skills and increased cooperation, the school staff wants to involve him in a regular physical education class. Games such as dodgeball are emphasized by the regular classroom teacher. For this reason, the physical education teacher selects dodgeball as the first game in which to involve the student.

Student Objective: To learn to play dodgeball.

Instructional Plan: Aware that the student uses his remaining sight to learn new tasks, the instructor selects demonstration, physical assistance, and word signs as the teaching strategies to emphasize. The plan is to familiarize the student with the game, boundaries, and equipment. Next, the instructor and a volunteer demonstrate the game. This is followed by the student's performing the game skills with the aid of the instructor (physical assistance) and the instructor's commentary (word signs).

Evaluation: It is obvious by the student's confused look and lack of attention that he does not understand the concept of the game as it is being demonstrated. The instructor determines that a second volunteer is needed to help give a more realistic demonstration of the game, as well as to free the instructor to be with the student to provide immediate feedback and physical assistance as needed.

Continued Instruction: Once a second volunteer is obtained by the teacher, efforts to teach the game of dodgeball are continued. Two volunteers and the instructor are able to provide an effective demonstration of how the game should be played. The instructor continues to stay close to the student, signing the appropriate action, and physically assisting the student to dodge the ball, retrieve the ball, roll the ball, etc. The teacher also provides immediate feedback relating to the success of the student's efforts. With this approach, the student quickly learns the elements of the game. Physical assistance is gradually eliminated, but appropriate word signs continue to be used during the flow of the game. Following these efforts, the student is successfully integrated into dodgeball games within the regular classroom's physical education program.

REFERENCES

Cowart, J. (1993). "Adapted Instructional and Equipment Ideas for Use with Pupils Who are Multihandicapped Blind Within a Leisure Time Context." In Jansma, P. (ed.), *The Psychomotor Domain and the Seriously Handicapped* (4th edition), 321-340. New York: University Press of America.

Fait, H. (1978). *Special Physical Education.* Philadelphia: W.B. Saunders.

Kelley, J. (1981). *Recreation Programming for Visually Impaired Children and Youth.* New York: American Foundation for the Blind.

Reams, D. (1980). *Project ComPAC.* Miami: Dade County Public Schools.

Sulzer-Azaroff, B., and Mayer, G. (1991). *Behavior Analysis for Lasting Change.* Fort Worth: Holt, Reinhart and Winston.

Vodola, T. (1973). *Individualized Physical Education Program for the Handicapped Child.* Englewood Cliffs, NJ: Prentice Hall.

Winnick, J. (1990). *Adapted Physical Education and Sport.* Champaign, IL: Human Kinetics.

SELECTED RESOURCES

Block, M.E. (1994). *A Teacher's Guide to Including Students with Disabilities in Regular Physical Education.* Baltimore, MD: Paul H. Brookes Publishing Co.

Docheff, D.M. (1990). "The Feedback Sandwich." *Journal of Physical Education, Recreation, and Dance*, **61**, 17-18.

Hsu, P-Y, and Dunn, J.M. (1984). "Comparing Reverse and Forward Chaining Instructional Methods on a Motor Task With Moderately Mentally Retarded Individuals." *Adapted Physical Education Quarterly*, **1**, 240-246.

Janes, R., and Dufek, J.S. (1993). "Movement Observation: What to Watch and Why." *Strategies*, **7**, 17-19.

Kratz, L.E., Tutt, L.M., and Block, D.A. (1987). *Movement and Fundamental Motor Skills for Sensory Deprived Children*. Springfield, IL: Charles C Thomas.

Nousner, L.D., and Griffey, D.C. (1994). "Wax On Wax Off: Pedagogical Content Knowledge in Motor Skill Instruction." *Journal of Health, Physical Education, Recreation and Dance*, **65**, 63-68.

Ormond, T.C. (1992). "The Prompt/Feedback Package in Physical Education." *Journal of Physical Education, Recreation and Dance*, **63**, 64-67.

Schuster, J.W., and Griffin, A.K. (1990). "Using Time Delay with Task Analysis." *Teaching Exceptional Children*, **22**, 49-53.

Spooner, F., Test, D.W., and Jolly, A.C. (1990). "Precision Teaching." *Teaching Exceptional Children*, **22**, 55-57.

Sprague, J.R., and Horner, R.H. (1990). "Easy Does It: Preventing Challenging Behaviors." *Teaching Exceptional Children*, **23**, 13-15.

Weber, R. (1989). "Motivating and Teaching Disabled Students: Using Task Variation in Adapted Physical Education." *Journal of Physical Education, Recreation and Dance*, **60**, 85-87.

Webster, G.E. (1993). "Effective Teaching in Adapted Physical Education . . . A Review." *Palaestra*, **9**, 25-31.

Part II

The Games

The Game Finder

USING THE GAME FINDER

The Game Finder that follows is designed to help you locate games and activities appropriate for your students. The following steps will help you use the Game Finder quickly and easily:

Step 1 — Use the Key on page 28 to identify the letters which correspond to whatever category and sport skill or physical and motor fitness skill you wish to emphasize.

Step 2 — Scan down the Category column in the Game Finder until you locate the letter representing your chosen category, then move to the right to see if the Sport Skills and Physical and Motor Fitness columns contain the appropriate letter(s) representing your desired sport skills or physical and motor fitness skill(s). (The Fundamental Motor Patterns and Skills column will have a check mark only if the game or activity includes these skills.)

Step 3 — Once you've found your category and corresponding skill, move to the left and note the name of the game or activity that incorporates the skill you wish to emphasize.

Step 4 — Refer to the corresponding page that is listed in the Game Finder and review in detail the game or activity to see if it will meet the students' needs. Each game or activity follows the same format.

The games and activities in this book are success oriented. All individuals should be able to participate within their ability. Remember that grade level is a suggested grade range. Aquatics activities may also have suggested grade ranges. Recreational activities can be used with either children or adults in educational or noneducational settings. Be flexible and creative when choosing equipment and setup to encourage successful participation, and to take advantage of whatever equipment you have at hand. If a game or activity is too easy for some, then you can add more challenging tasks. If a game or activity is difficult for others, use the suggestions listed in the adaptations section of the specific game or Part I of this book to ensure success for all individuals.

KEY

Category	Physical and Motor Fitness
E = Elementary School	Ag = Agility
M = Middle School	Ba = Balance
HS = High School	CR = Cardiorespiratory endurance
R = Recreation	ME = Muscular Endurance
Aq = Aquatics	F = Flexibility
	St = Muscular Strength
Sport Skills	***Fundamental Motor Patterns and Skills**
A = Archery	Examples include walking, running, hopping,
B = Baseball or Softball	skipping, sliding, galloping, etc.
Bb = Basketball	*Marked with a check.
Bo = Bowling	
C = Croquet	
Fb = Football	
Fr = Frisbee	
G = Golf	
Go = Goal Ball	
H = Hockey	
Hs = Horseshoes	
RS = Racquet Sports	
Ro = Roller Skating	
S = Soccer	
Sh = Showdown	
T = Track	
V = Volleyball	

GAME FINDER

Game Name	Category	Sport Skills	Physical & Motor Fitness	Fundamental Motor Patterns & Skills (✔)	Page
Airdyne Across (Insert your state name)	M, HS		CR	✔	66
Archery Balloon Pop	HS	A			81
Auditory Bowling	R	Bo			94
Ball in the Box or Goal	E,M		Ag,ME,St		34
Basketball Shoot	M,HS	Bb			68
Batting Skills (Lead-Up Game)	E,M	B,RS			69
Beach Ball Volleyball	HS	V	CR,ME		83
Beep Baseball	HS	B			84
Bell Balloon Bash	E	S	Ag,Ba,CR	✔	35
Bell Tetherball	R			✔	96
Body Painting	Aq		F		113
Bowling Pin Position	R	Bo			98
Box Ball or Bucket Ball	E		Ag,Ba,CR	✔	37
Bright Objects	E		Ag,Ba,CR	✔	38
Bucket Play	E,Aq		F		113
Busy Bee	E,M		Ag,Ba,CR	✔	40

Game Name	Category	Sport Skills	Physical & Motor Fitness	Fundamental Motor Patterns & Skills (✔)	Page
Call Ball or Spud	E,M		Ag,Ba	✔	60
Can Game	E,M			✔	71
Challenge Tasks	E		Ag,Ba	✔	41
Clean Up Your Room!	Aq		Ag,Ba,CR		114
Clothes Swim	Aq		CR,ME		116
Diamond Ball	E,M	B	St	✔	43
Duck Swim	Aq		CR,F,ME,St		117
Find the Ducky	E,Aq		CR		118
Fitness Wheel	R		CR,F,ME,St	✔	99
Flower Hunt	Aq		Ag,CR		119
Frisbee Bell Hockey	M,HS	H	Ag,Ba,CR,ME		86
Frisbee Golf	M,HS	Fr	CR		88
Goal Ball	M,HS	Go	Ag,CR,F,ME,St		91
Golden Sneaker Club	R	T	CR,ME		100
Holiday Roller Skating	R	Ro	Ag,Ba,CR,ME		101
Home Run Derby	HS	B			90
"I See"	E		Ag,Ba	✔	45
Jump Tag	E		Ag,Ba,St	✔	46
Kickball	E,M	B,S	CR	✔	47

Game Name	Category	Sport Skills	Physical & Motor Fitness	Fundamental Motor Patterns & Skills (✔)	Page
Lap Counting	Aq		CR,ME,St		120
Leader in the Circle	Aq				122
Modern Dance	HS		Ag,Ba,CR,F, ME	✔	93
Musical Hoops	Aq		CR,ME		123
Obstacle Course Ideas	E		Ag,Ba,St	✔	49
Parachute Pull	E,M		CR,St		50
Poison Ball	E		Ag,Ba,CR	✔	51
Poker Chip Pickup	E,M,HS		St		53
Pool Activities	E,Aq		Ag,Ba,CR,ME	✔	124
Pool Parachute	Aq		CR,F,St		125
Relays	E		Ag,Ba,CR,St	✔	54
Scatter Stations	R		Ag,Ba,CR,F, ME,St	✔	103
Scavenger Hunt	Aq		CR,F,St		127
Sensational Ping-Pong	R	RS	F,ME		104
Sequential Motor Patterns	E,M		Ag,Ba,CR,F, ME,St	✔	58
Shipwrecked	E		Ag,Ba,F,ME	✔	56
Showdown	R	Sh			105
Sockley	E,M	V,RS,B,S	Ag,CR,ME	✔	74

Game Name	Category	Sport Skills	Physical & Motor Fitness	Fundamental Motor Patterns & Skills (✔)	Page
Sponge Partners	Aq		CR		128
Stations	E	Bb,Bo	Ag,Ba	✔	61
Steal the Bacon	E,M	Bb,S	Ag,Ba	✔	76
Success-Oriented Horseshoes	R	Hs	St		107
Tactile T-Ball (Lead-Up Game)	M	B	F		78
Tactile Twister	R		Ba,F,ME,St		109
T-Ball	E,M	B			77
Team Cone Croquet	R	C			111
10 Shot	M,HS	Bb			65
Throw and Search	E,M	B		✔	63
Underwater Tag	Aq		CR,ME		131
Water Baseball	Aq	B	CR,ME		132
Water Soccer	Aq	S	CR,ME		134
Weather Game,The	Aq				130
Your Fitness Is in the Cards	E,M		CR,F,ME,St		72
Zone Volleyball	E,M	V	ME		79

Games
and Activities

The elementary years are a time for most children to acquire and/or refine their movement skills and patterns. To facilitate this skill development, children should have the opportunity to engage in a variety of movement activities and games. The basic movement skills and patterns learned at the elementary level are further refined and used in lead-up games, and activities of a more specialized nature, during the middle school years. At the high school level, students' skill emphasis and development is channeled even more into specific individual and group games and sports. Throughout all grade levels there are recreation and aquatics games and activities appropriate for all ages.

This section includes many activities and games with suggested adaptations that stress skill development at the elementary, middle, and high school levels as well as increased performance in recreation fitness and aquatics for *all* age groups. Note that *cardiorespiratory* is sometimes abbreviated *CR*.

GAME: CATEGORY:

BALL IN THE BOX OR GOAL   ELEMENTARY/MIDDLE SCHOOL

GOAL:
  To increase muscular strength and endurance and agility.

OBJECTIVE:
  Team members push their ball into the opposing team's box or goal.

EQUIPMENT:
  Two large colored boxes (one end of the box is open) or cones to mark goal areas, and two large balls at least 36 inches or larger in diameter.

SETUP:

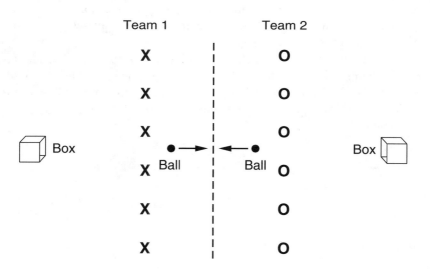

DESCRIPTION:
  First, familiarize team members with game equipment, boundaries, goal areas, etc. Next, position players on their respective starting lines. When the teacher gives the signal, team members push their ball toward the opposing team's box or goal area. The team that pushes its ball into the box or goal first, wins that round. Repeat play as long as time allows.

ADAPTATIONS:

■ A teacher, volunteer, or other assistant can help students push the ball, and where necessary, communicate game rules as well.

■ Use a caller or beeper at each box or goal to serve as a prompt for students who are visually impaired.

■ For safety, allow only three or four students to push the ball at once, depending upon the ability of the students.

INNOVATOR:

Doug Smith
Philip J. Rock Center and School

GAME:	CATEGORY:
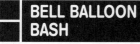 **BELL BALLOON BASH**	**ELEMENTARY SCHOOL**

GOAL:

To improve fundamental motor patterns and skills, agility, balance, cardiorespiratory (CR) endurance, and sport skills.

OBJECTIVE:

Each student follows his or her bell balloon around the gym with a previously chosen locomotor skill, and kicks the balloon when it is located.

EQUIPMENT:
Balloons with bells inside and a large gym floor.

SETUP:
Each student is given a balloon. Students with usable vision choose balloons of their favorite color.

DESCRIPTION:
Students kick the bell balloon and use the chosen locomotor skill (such as skipping, hopping, sliding, etc.) to locate the balloon and kick it again. It is suggested that the locomotor skill chosen be one that the student has already performed successfully. Be sure that any student who is totally blind is monitored for safety.

ADAPTATIONS:

▪ Using the chosen locomotor skill, students kick the balloon up to a cone and back to the starting line.

▪ Utilize sighted peer tutors as guides for students who are blind.

▪ Students can practice doing the locomotor skill fast or slow while going after the bell balloon.

■ Students can practice locating the balloon while changing from one locomotor skill to the other.

■ Use a big therapy ball instead of a bell balloon.

■ See how many times students can kick the balloon in a minute while using the chosen locomotor skill.

■ Have the students select the locomotor skill themselves.

■ Use a large balloon and have students in wheelchairs push themselves to the balloon, or have those using crutches ambulate to the balloon.

■ Have a teacher or volunteer assist students who are deaf and blind to locate the balloon.

INNOVATOR:

Lauren Lieberman
SUNY Brockport

GAME:	CATEGORY:
BOX BALL OR BUCKET BALL	**ELEMENTARY SCHOOL**

GOAL:

To improve agility, balance, CR endurance, and fundamental motor patterns and skills.

OBJECTIVE:

Students follow a sound source using a designated locomotor skill, pick up a ball, return to the starting line, and pass the ball down to the next person in the line.

EQUIPMENT:

Several small balls that can be hand held, buckets or boxes that are big enough to hold the balls, and a beeper or caller.

SETUP:

Organize an equal number of players on each team (three players on each team is ideal); have half of the teams on opposite ends of the room.

DESCRIPTION:

The players from each team are matched up according to similar abilities and assigned like numbers by the teacher. For example, both number 2s are students who are blind, both number 3s are partially sighted, etc. The teacher or volunteer stands between the two opposing teams with a box that contains the balls and the beeper. The teacher or volunteer calls out a number. The students who have been assigned that number travel in a prescribed manner (walk, jump, run, creep, bear walk, etc.) to the box, find a ball, and return it to their respective team. The activated beeper allows students who are blind to find the box with the balls, while teammates' voices provide a directional cue for the students' return. Upon reaching his or her team, the student passes the ball down the line of students to the last player. At this point the next number is called, and that student takes his or her turn. Play continues until all have had an opportunity to participate.

ADAPTATIONS:

■ The teacher can change the way the students pass the ball down the line; for example, pass the ball around the waist, touch the ball to the toes, pass the ball between the legs, etc.

■ Hold up cards with locomotor skills and/or numbers written on them to assist deaf children.

■ Have two or more students participate at the same time.

■ Students who are physically impaired and/or deaf-blind can be assisted, when necessary, by staff to perform the designated locomotor movement, carry the ball, and so forth.

■ Students with vision and/or hearing loss can use a cord taped to the floor, or a guide wire, as a guide to the box.

■ Students in wheelchairs can push forward, backward, fast, slow, and so forth to the box.

INNOVATORS:

Karen Allen and Stephen Kearney
Oklahoma School for the Blind

GAME:	CATEGORY:
BRIGHT OBJECTS	**ELEMENTARY SCHOOL**

GOAL:

To improve fundamental motor patterns and skills, agility, balance, and CR endurance.

OBJECTIVE:

Students perform a chosen locomotor skill to reach a bright object on the floor, pick it up, and take it to a designated area.

EQUIPMENT:

Beanbags, foam shapes, water balloons, and yarn balls (any group of objects from which the student would need to choose a specific color, shape, or size).

SETUP:

See below.

DESCRIPTION:

Several beanbags (or other objects) are placed around the players. The teacher then tells the students to perform the chosen locomotor skill to locate a beanbag and take it to a designated line or container. This sequence continues until all the beanbags have been picked up.

ADAPTATIONS:

■ Use a thematic approach, for example one in which apples are retrieved (harvest in the fall) and placed in a basket or bucket of water (include bobbing for apples when all have been retrieved). Other thematic ideas include "herding," in which pupils pick up stuffed animals and return them to the corrals; "parking cars," in which toy vehicles are retrieved and put in the parking lot ; or "picking flowers," in which students pick up bunches of plastic flowers and place them in vases, pots, etc.

■ Have each student refine previously learned skills or practice newly learned skills.

■ The students may have the objective of picking up all the round beanbags, all the red beanbags, all the small beanbags, etc.

■ Students who are blind can locate beanbags by following a cord on the floor, a sighted guide, or a sound source.

■ Staff can assist students who are deaf and blind or have multiple disabilities to move in the play area as needed.

INNOVATOR:
Lauren Lieberman
SUNY Brockport

GAME:	CATEGORY:
BUSY BEE	**ELEMENTARY/MIDDLE SCHOOL**

GOAL:
To improve fundamental motor patterns and skills, agility, balance, and CR endurance.

OBJECTIVE:
Students touch identified body parts on themselves or their partner; designated locomotor skills are used when finding a new partner.

EQUIPMENT:
None.

SETUP:
Divide the class into pairs. If there is an odd number, the instructor can play.

DESCRIPTION:
Each student faces his or her partner. One individual starts the activity by calling a body part—for example, hands to hands, nose to nose, elbow to elbow, etc. Partners in turn touch that body part. When the

caller calls "busy bee" everyone finds a new partner using designated locomotor skills, and the game begins again.

ADAPTATIONS:

■ A student who is deaf and blind can sign a body part to an oral peer or adult, who in turn verbalizes the direction to the rest of the class.

■ The speed at which the body parts are called can be increased as students become more proficient.

■ Discuss with the students any differences they noticed in their partners—for example, partner is shorter, partner's arms are longer, weight differences, etc.

■ Students who are physically impaired can participate within their ability.

■ A staff member or volunteer can sign the body parts to students who are deaf or deaf-blind.

■ When changing partners, have students utilize locomotor skills within their ability.

INNOVATOR:
Linda Gingery (retired)
Michigan School for the Blind

GAME:	CATEGORY:
CHALLENGE TASKS	**ELEMENTARY SCHOOL**

GOAL:
To improve fundamental motor patterns and skills, balance, and agility.

OBJECTIVE:
Students use basic movement skills in a variety of challenge tasks.

EQUIPMENT:
Depends on challenge tasks.

SETUP:
Students are spread out around the gym.

DESCRIPTION:
A major area of emphasis in physical education for young children who are visually impaired with multiple disabilities is to help them

develop their basic movement skills. In many cases it is necessary when teaching lower-functioning students to use the teaching strategies covered earlier as well as behavior modification. Once a student can comfortably perform movement patterns within his or her abilities, one must encourage the pupil to refine these patterns through such activities as challenge tasks in preparation for later participation in low-level organized games. Examples of challenge tasks for jumping (McClenaghan and Gallahue, 1978) are noted below:

Can you...
1. jump really low?
2. jump really high?
3. jump really far?
4. jump a short distance?
5. jump and land on your toes?
6. jump over a rope?
7. jump forward/backward?
8. jump with your feet close together?
9. jump with your feet far apart?

ADAPTATIONS:

■ Within the same challenge, allow each student to demonstrate the tasks within his or her capabilities.

■ Communicate with each child using his or her preferred means of communication.

■ If a student is having difficulty understanding or performing the tasks, use the most appropriate teaching strategy in order to assist the student to perform the desired movement.

INNOVATOR:

Jim Cowart
California School for the Blind

GAME:

CATEGORY:

DIAMOND
BALL

ELEMENTARY/MIDDLE
SCHOOL

GOAL:
To improve fundamental motor patterns and skills, baseball skills, and muscular strength.

OBJECTIVE:
Students hit the ball from a tee, then run the bases in the correct order.

EQUIPMENT:
- Five eye hooks
- Batting tee
- Yellow ski rope or equivalent
- Wiffle ball with bell pushed inside or beep baseball
- Oversized bat
- Rubber bases
- Athletic tape
- Large box or basket

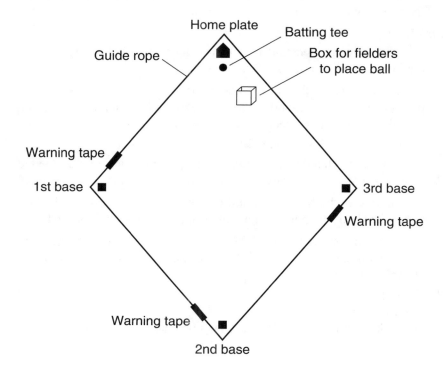

SETUP:

On gym walls, place eye hooks as noted in the diagram. Secure rope to each eye hook, forming the shape of a baseball or softball diamond. Place tape on the rope approximately 10-15 feet from each base; this serves as a warning to the base runner that he or she is approaching a base. Tape rubber bases to the floor in their proper places.

DESCRIPTION:

One of the hardest concepts for a number of blind children to understand is the baseball or softball "diamond." Diamond Ball was developed to help communicate this concept. Students are divided into hitting or fielding teams. Members of the fielding team are positioned in the field. When the ball is hit by a member of the hitting team from the tee, any player in the field may retrieve the ball. The object for the fielding team is to locate the ball and place it in a box located to the side of home plate as quickly as possible. Scoring for the batting team occurs in the following way: After hitting the ball from the tee, the batter grasps the guide rope and runs to first base; if he or she reaches the base before the ball is placed in the box adjacent to home plate, one point is scored. If the base runner reaches second base before the ball is placed in the box, two points are scored; three points are awarded for a triple, and a home run is worth four points for the batting team. When everyone on the batting team has batted, the teams switch positions. Points earned are tallied for each team.

ADAPTATIONS:

■ The use of a rubber mat to stand on when batting helps students who are blind establish a sense of direction.

■ If a beep baseball is not available, bells placed inside a Wiffle ball provide an adequate sound substitute for the fielding team; in addition, verbal prompts will be necessary to aid students who are blind to locate a stationary ball in the playing field or on the batting tee.

■ A teacher, an aide, or a volunteer can provide assistance as needed when students who are physically impaired are batting, fielding, etc.

■ Students who have more abilities may swing at a pitched ball on either the fly or the bounce if a playground or soccer ball is used.

■ If eye hooks are not available to secure the guide rope to the wall, check with the school's maintenance staff for another method of attaching the rope.

INNOVATOR:

Candice Rehmeier
Nebraska School for the Visually Handicapped

GAME:	CATEGORY:
"I SEE"	**ELEMENTARY SCHOOL**

GOAL:
To improve fundamental motor patterns and skills, agility, and balance.

OBJECTIVE:
Students listen to directions and perform designated movements and balance tasks.

EQUIPMENT:
None unless stated objective requires.

DESCRIPTION:
The activity is started by the teacher saying, "I see." Students reply, "What do you see?" If the emphasis of the lesson is on basic movement skills, the teacher may respond, for example, "I see boys and girls *jumping* up and down" or "I see boys and girls *crawling* around on the floor." For body awareness, the response could be, "I see boys and girls touching *ankle to ankle*!" The students in turn perform the designated activities. The possibilities are limitless!

ADAPTATIONS:
■ Allow the students to be callers. Students who are deaf or deaf-blind can sign the tasks to an adult or peer who in turn gives verbal direction.

■ Be sure to include some creative directives to make it fun, such as "I see students creeping like bears" or "I see students squirming like snakes."

■ Using cones or chairs, incorporate concepts such as front, back, left, and right.

■ Have students pair up to play "I See." For example, one partner is the caller, and the other is the performer, then switch.

■ Provide assistance to students who are physically challenged as needed to perform a skill or substitute skill. Instead of crawling on the floor, for example, a student in a wheelchair can move the chair in a zigzag pattern.

■ Give a response that allows each student to perform the task within his or her capabilities—for example, "I see some students jumping and others creeping."

SUBMITTED BY:
Candice Rehmeier
Nebraska School for the Visually Handicapped

GAME:	CATEGORY:
JUMP TAG	**ELEMENTARY SCHOOL**

GOAL:
To improve fundamental motor patterns and skills, agility, balance, and muscular strength.

OBJECTIVE:
Students use basic movement skills either to avoid being tagged by "it" or, if student is "it," to try to tag other students.

EQUIPMENT:
Gym walls and mats used for activity boundries and mini beeper.

SETUP:
One player is selected as "it"; the remaining players are scattered within the playing area. The only way a player can move around the playing area is by jumping (forward, backward, or sideways).

DESCRIPTION:
Each game consists of a few minutes; during this time, "it" attempts to tag the other players; a player can be touched more than once during the game. After a player is tagged, the players spread out over the playing area before play is again started. The object of the game is for players to be tagged as few times as possible by "it". The player having been tagged the least number of times during the game becomes "it" for the next game. To add interest to the game, some players like to include a "safe" position. This is a position players can assume twice during the game and not be tagged by "it". Players can get very creative in determining the types of positions that can be considered "safe."

ADAPTATIONS:
■ Skills and movements used in a tag game are limited only by the teachers' and players' creativity and imagination. Players can be requested to perform other previously learned skills such as hopping, skipping, galloping, etc.; various animal walks can be emphasized, such as the crab walk or elephant walk; players can pull or push themselves when prone, supine, kneeling, or sitting on a scooter board.

- For students who are blind with hearing, "it" wears a mini beeper that emits an intermittent sound; in turn, the other players regularly call "it's" name. In this way, the players who are blind know the general location of each other.

- For students with some vision and hearing, have "it" wear a blindfold.

- If "it" is deaf with some sight, have him or her perform a more difficult skill that restricts movement, or blindfold the player and have an adult or sighted peer hold his or her arm or hand.

- For deaf-blind students, have an adult or sighted peer hold the student's hand or arm.

- Students with multiple disabilities (unable to move in designated way) can be asked to perform a movement skill within their ability.

- Examples of "safe" positions suggested by students include hugging another student, squatting with hands touching the feet, etc. The position can be maintained for a count of five. (Students count out loud.)

- An alternative way to free a tagged player is to have the tagged player do a designated number of exercises or stunts before resuming play.

INNOVATOR:
Jim Cowart
California School for the Blind

GAME:	CATEGORY:
KICKBALL	**ELEMENTARY/MIDDLE SCHOOL**

GOAL:
To improve fundamental motor skills and patterns, CR endurance, and sport skills.

OBJECTIVE:
Students play a modified version of kickball.

SETUP:
Students are divided into two teams.

DESCRIPTION:

The student who is "up" kicks the ball as far as he or she can and runs the bases as fast as possible. The fielder who retrieves the ball immediately starts to bounce the ball a predetermined number of times—15, 20, 25, depending on the ability of the base runner. When the ball is bounced the required number of times the base runner has to stop. If the base runner reaches first base, he or she receives one point, second base two points, third base three points, etc. There are no outs; each player on the team has the opportunity to be "up" once or twice, depending upon the time allotted for the game, before teams change positions. When all players have had the opportunity to be up the predetermined amount of times, the teams switch positions.

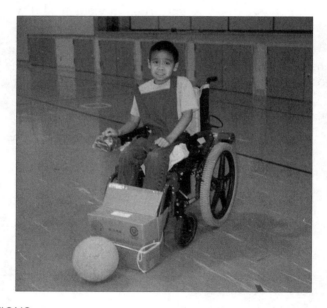

ADAPTATIONS:

■ Have *all* the outfielders bounce the ball a designated number of times—say, 5 or 10—before the base runner must stop.

■ Use guide runners for students who are blind, deaf-blind, or have physical disabilities.

■ Use peer pushers or aides for students in wheelchairs who are unable to push their own chairs.

■ Have students keep their own scores.

■ A student who is unable to stand and dribble the ball on the ground can sit or kneel and dribble. The student could also do a predetermined number of air dribbles, passes around the body, or passes between the legs.

■ Students who are deaf-blind or physically disabled can be provided assistance as needed when kicking, running bases, fielding, and so on.

■ Students with physical involvement may "kick" the ball using any method within their ability—for example, use the hands, arms, or head.

INNOVATOR:

John Schrock
Missouri School for the Blind

GAME:	CATEGORY:
OBSTACLE COURSE IDEAS	**ELEMENTARY SCHOOL**

GOAL:

To improve fundamental motor patterns and skills, agility, strength, and balance.

OBJECTIVE:

Students have multiple opportunities to practice the skills needed to correctly complete the obstacle course.

EQUIPMENT:

Several pieces of equipment to challenge individual students are noted below. Options are sufficient to allow the instructor to select items to fit any available space.

SETUP:

Set up equipment in a circle or "U" formation so students can more easily go from one obstacle to the next and return to start.

DESCRIPTION:

Sample stations and skill/activities:

1. Two cones, with soft cotton rope tied to Nerf balls that are pulled into the cones; this serves as an obstacle to jump over, step over, and so forth.

2. Chairs or cones used for an agility run.

3. A trapezoid cube bolster to crawl through.

4. A small crash pad for balance and tumbling skills.

5. Three tunnels in a row for moving through or over.

6. A sturdy cardboard box used as a tunnel.

7. A low, sturdy table covered by a long, thick mat to create a "mountain" for climbing.

8. A wooden A-frame climber for balance or climbing tasks.

9. A low balance beam for stationary or dynamic balance stunts.

SUGGESTIONS:

1. Use each station as an activity center, so only two or three students are using it at a time, resulting in little waiting and lots of activity.

2. Arrange equipment to emphasize concepts such as up, down, under, over, etc.

3. To ensure safety, always designate a time when the next person can start. For example: "When the person ahead of you has climbed down the climber, or stepped off the balance beam, then you may begin."

ADAPTATIONS:

■ Place a sighted student peer with a student who is blind so the two can move together between stations.

■ Stations may be added, deleted, or changed, or skills may be performed more slowly or in parts to accommodate students who are physically involved or deaf-blind.

INNOVATOR:

Sue Fleming
Sitka, Alaska

GAME:	CATEGORY:
PARACHUTE PULL	**ELEMENTARY/MIDDLE SCHOOL**

GOAL:

To increase muscular strength and cardiovascular endurance.

OBJECTIVE:

A group of approximately five students pulls one student sitting on a parachute.

EQUIPMENT:

Parachute (full size).

SETUP:

Gym or long corridor.

DESCRIPTION:

One student sits on the parachute. The other pupils stand facing the seated student and roll the parachute into their hands. Once ready, students pull the parachute walking backward, with guidance from adults, the length of the gym or corridor. At the end, another student sits on the parachute while the rest of the students pull him or her in the other direction.

ADAPTATIONS:

■ Some students may need physical prompts in order to pull appropriately.

■ A staff member may need to assist students who may lose their balance while pulling.

■ For some students, the use of single words may be more understandable—for example, "Your turn," "Sit," "Pull," "Stand up," "Walk back." For other pupils it may be necessary to use sign language.

■ Students with physical disabilities or who are deaf-blind, may need assistance to assume a safe acceptable position on the parachute as well as when pulling the chute.

■ Most elementary texts include parachute activities emphasizing strength development that can be used with the above activity.

INNOVATOR:

Doug Smith
Philip J. Rock Center and School

GAME:	CATEGORY:
POISON BALL	**ELEMENTARY SCHOOL**

GOAL:

To develop and refine fundamental motor patterns and skills, practice balance and agility tasks, and improve CR endurance.

OBJECTIVE:

Students move away in different ways from the sound of a bouncing ball.

EQUIPMENT:

Playground ball or cage ball.

SETUP:

Students scatter around the gym.

DESCRIPTION:

The instructor or student bounces the playground or cage ball around the gym and tries to touch students with his or her hand. The students move away from the sound of the ball and try not to be touched by the person with the ball. Students touched by this person have several options: They may accumulate points, do a specific number of exercises before again participating, "freeze" until freed by an untagged player (yelling "help" to attract an untagged player), etc.

ADAPTATIONS:

■ If the student with the ball cannot see the other pupils, have the students clap hands, call out his or her name, shake bells, or the like.

■ Students can employ various movements: scoot, jump, walk, run, push wheelchair, and so forth. Have students perform skills within their ability.

■ Have a student or students be the "tagger."

■ The instructor or student can wear a beeper instead of bouncing the ball, and move around the room trying to tag the players.

■ Students who are totally blind or who have limited mobility can be paired with a peer partner.

■ Provide assistance to students who are deaf-blind and with multiple disabilities so they can safely move around the gym, perform designated tasks (or substituted tasks) after being tagged, understand rules of the game, and so forth.

INNOVATOR:

Linda Gingery (retired)
Michigan School for the Blind

GAME:

POKER CHIP PICKUP

CATEGORY:

ELEMENTARY/MIDDLE/ HIGH SCHOOL

GOAL:
To improve strength.

OBJECTIVE:
Students utilize upper body strength to raise and lower parachute then locate objects on the floor using appropriate searching techniques.

EQUIPMENT:
Parachute, poker chips, paper cups.

SETUP:
Students stand in a circle, holding the edge of the parachute with both hands.

DESCRIPTION:
Students raise and lower the parachute on command—for example, "Up 1-2-3, down 1-2-3." Poker chips are then placed in the parachute and students raise and lower the parachute until all poker chips have fallen out of the parachute. Students are then given a paper cup to collect the fallen poker chips.

ADAPTATIONS:
- Students can work as partners to locate the chips.
- The class can be divided into teams.
- Use other objects such as beanbags, coins, peanuts, shells, etc.
- Staff or volunteers can assist students who have physical disabilities or who are deaf-blind to manipulate the chute, collect chips, communicate directions, and the like.

INNOVATOR
Linda Gingery (retired)
Michigan School for the Blind

GAME:	CATEGORY:
RELAYS	**ELEMENTARY SCHOOL**

GOAL:
To improve fundamental motor patterns and skills, agility, balance, CR endurance, and strength.

OBJECTIVE:
Students perform designated skills.

EQUIPMENT:
- Cones: color-coded for ease of identification by students who are visually impaired.
- Floor tape
- 6-inch pieces of dowel (broom handle)
- Jump ropes
- Hoops
- Scooters: preferably 24 to 30 inches long
- Batons (plastic wrap tubes)
- Tennis balls
- Beanbags

SETUP:
1. Use the width of the gym (frequency of turns is preferable to distance covered).

2. Use floor tape to mark the starting line and place cones across the gym as turning points.

3. Color-coded cones serve as directional cues for students with some vision; beepers can be used for students who are blind, and cord can be taped to the floor for students who are deaf-blind.

4. Utilize two students per team. Each pair (team) stands on the starting line opposite their cone.

5. Tasks are repeated for a designated number of times or for a set time limit.

DESCRIPTION:
Examples of locomotor skills:

■ Run around the cone and back, then tag the partner. (If necessary, substitute a locomotor skill within the student's ability.)

■ Run around the cone carrying a baton, and pass the baton to the partner.

■ Run to the cone, drop a 6-inch dowel into the hole at the top of the cone, retrieve it from under the cone, and return it to partner.

■ Jump rope to the cone and return. (If student is unable to jump rope, he or she may step over the rope as it is turned while moving forward.)

■ Walk around the cone and back with beanbag on the head.

■ Run forward carrying a tennis ball and place it on top of the cone; run back and touch starting line; run again to retrieve the ball before giving it to the partner, who is waiting at the starting point.

Examples of scooter activities:

■ Push or pull oneself with the hands while prone, or sit on the scooter and pull and push oneself with the legs.

■ Partners: One student sits on the scooter board while the other student pushes on the rider's shoulders; the rider needs to steer with his or her feet and/or use the feet as a bumper.

■ Partners sit back to back; using their feet, one pushes while the other pulls.

ADAPTATIONS:

■ A taller cone may be easier to find for students with some sight.

■ Directional cues for students who are blind may include a beeper at the cone and the partner's voice at the starting line.

■ Students who are blind may be able to better hear directional cues when they participate at one end of the gym.

■ Assistance can be provided to students with multiple disabilities or who are deaf-blind to utilize scooter boards, perform locomotor skills, and so forth.

■ The instructor can be creative in the movement skills that he or she asks students to perform.

INNOVATOR:

Sue Fleming
Sitka, Alaska

GAME:	CATEGORY:
SHIPWRECKED	**ELEMENTARY SCHOOL**

GOAL:

To improve flexibility, balance, agility, muscular endurance, and fundamental motor patterns and skills.

OBJECTIVE:

Students listen for the captain's (a teacher or student) commands and respond appropriately.

EQUIPMENT:

Gym.

SETUP:

Students scatter around the gym.

DESCRIPTION:

The captain of the ship gives the commands, and the students perform the designated tasks. The game is fast-moving and requires the students to listen and follow directions.

COMMANDS–TASKS

1. "Ship's bow" (or stern, port, etc.)—students run forward (for kindergarten students, use "front of ship," "back of ship," etc.).

2. "Torpedo"—students place their hands together overhead and run around the gym.

3. "Hit the deck"—students lie down flat.

4. "Abandon ship"—in pairs, students simulate a rowing motion.

5. "Man overboard"—students place a hand over their brow to shade sunshine and look to the right and left.

6. "Cook's in the galley"—students get into groups of three or four sitting in a circle.

7. "Swab the deck"—students simulate a swaying motion with their arms and body, like mopping.

8. "To the crow's nest"—students pretend they are climbing a ladder.

9. "Man the pumps"—students get into a push-up position and do push-ups.

10. "Bring in the anchor"—students pretend they are pulling in an anchor.

ADAPTATIONS:

■ Use the wall as a guide when moving to the front or back of the ship. Secure tape or a rope to the walls 6 feet from each end to signal the end of the gym or room.

■ Use another student or a volunteer as a helper for students who are blind, deaf-blind, or with physical disabilities to assist in understanding commands and performing tasks (substitute skills). It may be necessary to familiarize students with the commands and movements during the first few sessions.

■ Call out "torpedo" when running to spread everyone out, and then give another command.

INNOVATOR:

Sue Fleming
Sitka, Alaska

GAME:	CATEGORY:
SEQUENTIAL MOTOR PATTERNS	**ELEMENTARY/MIDDLE SCHOOL**

GOAL:
To develop balance, agility, flexibility, strength, fundamental motor patterns and skills, and CR and muscular endurance.

OBJECTIVE:
Students move from station to station achieving their best motoric performance on each obstacle.

EQUIPMENT:
Large sponge donut, conventional gym mat, decline/incline wedge mat, balance beam, horizontal ladder, large blocks placed like steps, hula hoops, an accordion tunnel, and similar objects.

SETUP:
Arrange the following stations in a circle.

DESCRIPTION:
Sample stations:

1. Creep or crawl through the donut.

2. Perform log, forward, or back rolls or animal walks up and down the mat.

3. Log roll or forward roll a specific number of times on the mat.

4. Start on all fours, then stand up; repeat a specific number of times.

5. Step over the rungs of the ladder or walk forward, sideways, or backward on the sides of the ladder.

6. With the balance beam positioned on the floor, walk sideways, forward, backward, etc.

7. Walk up and down steps or large blocks.

8. Walk, jump, or hop from one hula hoop to the other.

9. Jump inside the hula hoop.

10. Finish with appropriate gross motor exercises (i.e., sit-ups, squat thrust, V-sit, static stretches, etc.).

ADAPTATIONS:
■ Familiarize students who are blind or deaf-blind with the stations.

■ Provide physical assistance when necessary to perform skills, change stations, and so on.

■ For students who have a hearing loss or are deaf-blind, communicate desired tasks and directions with sign.

■ Have students go through the course for time, emphasizing individual improvement. (Eliminate time if there is a potential for injury or a student performs skills poorly in an attempt to gain time.)

■ Have the students perform the activity or skill within their ability.

■ Vary stations to maintain student interest.

■ Increase or decrease the number of stations, depending upon the ability level of students.

■ Design stations and tasks to challenge each student's skill level. For example, one student may be challenged by crawling through the tunnel forward while another is challenged crawling backward, etc.

INNOVATOR:
John Schrock
Missouri School for the Blind

GAME:	CATEGORY:
CALL BALL OR SPUD	**ELEMENTARY/MIDDLE SCHOOL**

GOAL:
To improve fundamental motor patterns and skills, agility, and balance.

OBJECTIVE:
A student retrieves a bouncing ball and hits a classmate by rolling the ball.

EQUIPMENT:
Ball (bell ball, beeper ball, playground ball).

SETUP:
The students gather in the middle of the room.

DESCRIPTION:
One person has the ball and throws it up above his or her head with two hands and calls a person's name. The person called has to locate the bouncing ball and call "spud" when it is in his or her possession. The other students scatter around the gym and keep moving until they hear the word "spud." When the students hear "spud," they stand in place and

clap their hands. The person with the ball rolls it at a clapping player and tries to hit his or her legs. A student who is hit with the ball is assigned a score of one potato. A player who receives a third potato must execute a designated task (e.g., animal walk). Once completed, the student then reenters the game. After a player is hit, the ball is given to another classmate, who continues the game.

ADAPTATIONS:

■ When necessary, assign each student who is blind or deaf-blind a sighted guide. Also provide an aid when necessary for each student with a physical disability. They can assist students to move appropriately, roll the ball, clap at a designated time, and so on.

■ Use more than one ball at a time.

■ The game can be played with partners.

INNOVATOR:

Linda Gingery (retired)
Michigan School for the Blind

GAME:	CATEGORY:
STATIONS	**ELEMENTARY SCHOOL**

GOAL:

To improve balance, agility, fundamental motor patterns and skills, and sport skills.

OBJECTIVE:

Students go from station to station performing the predetermined skill and/or activity to their best ability.

EQUIPMENT:

(Specific to the station chosen—see below.)
Digital kitchen timer—to remind teacher and students when to rotate stations.

SETUP:

Listed below are a variety of items to choose from:

1. Hula hoops—free play.

2. Bowling—one to ten pins (mark spots on floor), a 10-inch playground ball, and balance beams or two-by-fours on the floor to separate lanes.

3. Hoops suspended from the ceiling or an overhead ladder or the like, with a bell or milk jug (with unpopped popcorn inside) attached to the hoop to give feedback regarding the success of a thrown ball; use light 10-inch slow motion (Slo-Mo) balls or Nerf balls for throwing. (Slo-Mo balls from Sportime in Appendix D.)

4. Basketball hoop attached to a wall, pole, or the like (height depends on ability level of the student); use mini basketballs, playground balls, or the like.

5. Scooter board obstacle course—use folded mats, cones, tunnels, chairs, etc. as obstacles. (For example, two chairs with plastic or a bamboo sticks across the seats or a low table can be used as a tunnel.)

6. Jump ropes—have a variety of tasks to challenge students' abilities, from simply jumping over a rope on the floor to independently using a jump rope.

7. Beanbag toss—have milk crates or hoops on the floor or wall.

8. Chin bar—chin-ups, hang for time, and so forth.

DESCRIPTION:
Students are shown or demonstrated the expected skill to perform at each station. They are then assigned a place to begin. Stations are numbered or color-coded. When it is time to change stations, one approach may be to say, "Stop, put your equipment away. Red (station students) go to Blue, Blue go to Yellow," and so on.

ADAPTATIONS:
■ Gradually increase the length and complexity of the course depending on the students' ability.

■ It may be necessary to familiarize students who are blind or deaf-blind with the various stations or skills prior to the class. In this way, there will be less delay in starting the activity.

■ Place beepers on targets for directional cues.

■ Have a teacher, aide, or peer assist in aligning the pupils for throws, retrieving balls or equipment, performing skills, moving to stations, and so forth.

■ Use the appropriate level of assistance to teach the skills.

■ Have a student perform an activity or skill within his or her ability if the designated skill is inappropriate.

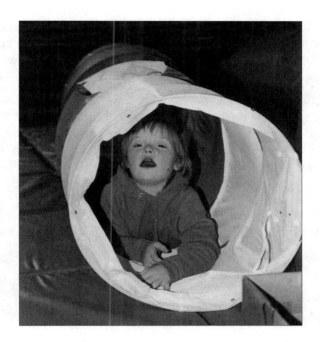

INNOVATOR:
Sue Fleming
Sitka, Alaska

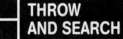

GAME:	CATEGORY:
THROW AND SEARCH	**ELEMENTARY/MIDDLE SCHOOL**

GOAL:
To improve fundamental motor patterns and skills and sport skills.

OBJECTIVE:
Students throw beanbags at a target using the one-handed underhand throw.

EQUIPMENT:
Mat, beanbags; target objects such as pie tins, bells, wind chimes, or tin cans.

SETUP:

Hang target objects from old venetian blinds, overhead ladders, stall bars, and the like. Place a mat 5-10 feet from the hanging objects.

DESCRIPTION:

Students square their heels to the mat for alignment. Give each student 10 beanbags; students throw the beanbags at the hanging objects, using the underhand throw. The beanbags hitting the objects will give auditory feedback. After all students have taken their turn, students locate the beanbags by sweeping their hands slowly across the floor under the target objects. When all bags have been collected, repeat the activity.

ADAPTATIONS:

- Decrease or increase the distance between the mat and the objects.

- Arrange targets from low to high.

- Vary the throw: two-handed underhand throw, chest pass, bounce pass, and so on.

- A flashlight attached to the target can provide a directional cue for students with limited vision.

■ For students who are deaf-blind, use sign language to communicate rules, successes, and so forth.

■ Provide physical assistance as needed for students having difficulty executing a throw—for example, by modifying the throwing pattern.

INNOVATOR:
Linda Gingery (retired)
Michigan School for the Blind

GAME:	CATEGORY:
10 SHOT	**MIDDLE/HIGH SCHOOL**

GOAL:
To improve sport skills (basketball).

OBJECTIVE:
Students execute foul shots using a two-handed underhand shot, one-handed set shot, or two-handed set shot.

EQUIPMENT:
Basketballs, baskets, and backboards with an auditory unit behind or on the backboards (when possible), and mats.

SETUP:
Place mats in front of the baskets with one of the short ends of each mat on the foul line or closer.

DESCRIPTION:
When shooting, a student faces the basketball hoop with heels against the front edge of the mat. He or she shoots a series of 10 consecutive shots; each student keeps track of his or her score, utilizing the following scoring system:

■ One point if ball hits the backboard

■ Two points if ball hits the rim

■ Three points if ball goes in basket

Students challenge themselves by attempting to exceed their previous best score.

ADAPTATIONS:

■ Use a lighter ball (playground ball, volley ball, etc.) for younger students if necessary.

■ The game can be played in teams. If a team is short of players, staff or volunteers can be blindfolded and participate on that team.

■ Move students closer to the basket or farther away depending upon ability.

■ Try to have available adjustable baskets that can be lowered for pupils unable to reach a standard basketball hoop.

■ Provide assistance as needed to students who have multiple disabilities or are deaf-blind in order for them to successfully execute foul shots, keep score, rebound the ball, and so forth.

■ Tap the rim with a pole to provide a directional cue.

INNOVATOR:

Linda Gingery (retired) contributed the game, though the true innovator is unknown.

Michigan School for the Blind

GAME:	CATEGORY:
AIRDYNE ACROSS (INSERT YOUR STATE NAME)	**MIDDLE/ HIGH SCHOOL**

GOAL:

To develop cardiorespiratory endurance and fundamental motor patterns and skills.

OBJECTIVE:

Each student rides a stationary bicycle or Airdyne bicycle (student uses arms as well as legs) at a constant pace for a designated time. Students select cities or towns within the state, locate the mileage to each, and choose an interesting fact about each place.

EQUIPMENT:

Airdyne or stationary exercise bicycles, and a large outline of the state noting selected towns and cities.

SETUP:

Have available stationary bicycles within the gym, weight room, or classroom.

DESCRIPTION:

Students ride three to five times per week to accumulate miles. This is an activity in which all students with sensory impairments will be able to participate equally. Before starting, the student must:

1. Decide whether to accumulate mileage individually or as a team.

2. Determine the towns and cities to visit.

3. Locate mileage to the identified towns or cities.

Once the above decisions have been made, students keep track of miles biked. These figures are recorded on the large state map. When students reach their destination, they are responsible for collecting historical information about the town or city. They then present this information to the entire class. The activity has proven to be very motivating for the students.

ADAPTATIONS:

■ This activity can be adapted to any group. Younger children can participate by walking, running, jumping rope, etc. The activity can be converted to miles any number of ways; one trip around the school yard equals 1 mile, 10 jumps with a rope equals 1 mile, and so on. The level of information gathered can be adjusted for the age level or ability of the student(s).

■ Outline the state map, and note distances to the chosen towns and cities using thickly painted string (place a piece of string in wet paint, and let it dry). Students use their sense of touch to get an idea of the shape of the state as well as the distance to various towns and cities.

■ Students unable to bike may accumulate miles by walking, wheeling, rolling, and so forth.

■ The mileage of slower students may be multiplied by 2, 5, or 10, depending upon the need.

■ Students can keep track of their miles on a computer, graph, map, chart, or the like.

INNOVATOR:

Candice Rehmeier
Nebraska School for the Visually Handicapped

GAME:	CATEGORY:
BASKETBALL SHOOT	**MIDDLE/ HIGH SCHOOL**

GOAL:
Improve sport skills (basketball).

OBJECTIVE:
Students take turns passing, running, shooting, and rebounding.

EQUIPMENT:
Basketballs, baskets, cones, and a backboard with a beeper attached (when possible).

SETUP:
Place a cone in the area of each foul line, closer to or farther from the basket depending upon the ability of the student. Have teams of two or three students; each team lines up facing a basket.

DESCRIPTION:
The first person in line has a basketball. The game begins when the teacher says "go." The first person passes the ball overhead to the person behind. The second student runs to the cone and shoots at the basket. He or she rebounds the ball and returns to the front of the line. Immediately he or she passes the ball to the next person, who continues the drill until stopped by the teacher.

ADAPTATIONS:

▪ Keep points—one for hitting the backboard or rim, and two for a basket.

▪ Use the game as a relay or shooting drill.

▪ Add a dribble up to the cone instead of running with the ball.

▪ Change positions of the teams and cones so students learn to shoot from different angles and distances.

▪ Use a beeper or other sound cue (hand clap, verbal directive, etc.) to indicate the location of the basket or cone, positions of teammates, and so on.

▪ Have adjustable baskets to accommodate students unable to reach a standard basketball hoop.

▪ For students with multiple disabilities, a staff member may need to provide assistance to locate the cones and/or basket, execute a shot, rebound the ball, return to team members, and so forth.

▪ Have students pass the ball under the legs or around the body.

▪ Use a ball other than a basketball.

▪ Give students more than one turn.

INNOVATOR:

Linda Webbert
Maryland School for the Blind

GAME:	CATEGORY:
BATTING SKILLS (LEAD-UP GAME)	**ELEMENTARY/MIDDLE SCHOOL**

GOAL:

To improve sport skills (baseball).

OBJECTIVE:

Students stand individually or with a partner and practice tracking and batting balls.

EQUIPMENT:

Rope and string (or fishing line); bats, paddles, or racquets (any object used to hit a ball); Wiffle ball, balloon, beach ball, baseball, softball, or a like object to strike; and a batting tee and/or designated pitcher who can pitch for successful batting.

SETUP:

At a few stations tie strings to the balls, balloons, or other objects and hang them from the ceiling, an overhead ladder, or a rope suspended between tetherball or volleyball standards. Put batting tees at other stations with different-sized balls. At the remaining stations place a home plate where students will stand to hit a pitched ball.

DESCRIPTION:

Initially, have each student practice the striking skill while emphasizing stance, weight transfer, tracking, and contact points. Then have students pair up and take turns hitting objects at different stations. Ask challenging questions such as "How many times in a row can you hit the ball?" or "Can you hit it within three pitches?"

ADAPTATIONS:

■ Lower the objects on the strings, and practice kicking skills.

■ Raise the objects on the strings, and work on the overhand throw or serving motion.

■ Put bells in the balls or balloons used by students with visual impairments. Use bright balls and balloons for students with low vision.

■ Provide assistance to students having difficulty performing the striking skill.

■ Make the balls softer or harder depending upon the need.

■ Increase or decrease the size of the striking object depending upon the ability of the student.

■ For students who are deaf or deaf-blind, provide communication assistance to increase their knowledge of the proper striking stance.

INNOVATOR:

Monica Kleeman
Perkins School for the Blind

GAME:	CATEGORY:
CAN GAME	**ELEMENTARY/MIDDLE SCHOOL**

GOAL:

To improve fundamental motor patterns and skills.

OBJECTIVE:

Students execute an overhand and underhand throw at a designated target for distance and/or accuracy.

EQUIPMENT:

Hula hoops, 10 or more empty soda cans per hula hoop, and five or more beanbags per student.

SETUP:

Place hula hoops on the floor or ground with cans inside each hoop. Students stand a challenging distance away from the soda cans.

DESCRIPTION:

This can be an individual or group activity. Give each student five or more beanbags. The instructor, peer tutors, or volunteers tap the soda cans to cue the students where to throw. The students in turn throw the beanbags at the soda cans using either an overhand or underhand throw, attempting to knock over as many as possible. After each throw students are told the number of cans hit. Students keep their own scores and/or a group score. The staff may return the beanbags by sliding them on the floor to the students' feet.

ADAPTATIONS:

■ Place the soda cans (targets) on tables to encourage students to aim higher.

■ Move the students farther away for a greater challenge.

■ Students can utilize different throws such as sidearm, underhand, or overhand.

■ Students who are blind or deaf-blind may need a staff person to help position them in preparation for their throws, assist them to "feel" how far away the cans are before throwing, keep score, give feedback on their throws, and so on.

■ Place beepers adjacent to hula hoops as a directional cue.

INNOVATOR:

Beth Hudy
Royer Greaves School for the Blind

GAME: CATEGORY:

**YOUR FITNESS IS
IN THE CARDS**

**ELEMENTARY/MIDDLE
SCHOOL**

GOAL:

To increase cardiorespiratory endurance, flexibility, and muscular strength and endurance.

OBJECTIVE:

Students read the cards dealt to them at the beginning of the "warm-up" period and correctly execute the corresponding exercises noted on the chart.

EQUIPMENT:

A deck of cards or brailled cards and a label maker (braille) chart noting the exercise/activity for each card, mats, jump ropes, carpet squares, a climbing rope, and weight equipment.

SETUP:

Set up stations in gym area (see next page).

DESCRIPTION:

This is a fun warm-up activity. Students receive five playing cards when entering the gym. The students must look at their cards and consult the exercise/activity chart (or have a staff member do it for them) to find out what corresponding exercises or activities they must do and the correct number of repetitions at each station. These stations (and chart) may be changed to reflect the students' skills. Stations may emphasize "fitness" and, for example, have the following activities/exercises:

- An "ace" = jog four laps around the gym.
- A "king" = 20 sit-ups.
- A "queen" = 25 jumping jacks.
- A "jack" = 10 jumps using a weighted jump rope.
- A "joker" = the student must pull him or herself on a carpet square two times across the gym floor.
- Hearts numbered 10 and under = the student must jump rope the number on the card multiplied by itself (i.e., eight of hearts = 8 x 8 = 64 jumps).
- Spades numbered 10 and under = the student must perform the same number of repetitions of push-ups as the number on the card.
- Diamonds numbered 10 and under = the student must perform the same number of repetitions of leg lifts on the weight machine as the number on the card.
- Clubs numbered 10 and under = the number of times a student must hang on a climbing rope for 15 counts each time.

ADAPTATIONS:

- Construct a brailled or large-print master chart illustrating the meaning of each playing card.
- Use brailled playing cards.
- A sighted guide and/or indoor guide wires can be used by the students when running laps.
- Set up stations in the same area when repeating this warm-up activity.
- Adaptations should be made on the chart for students who have multiple disabilities. (Each station could have three or four options.)
- Provide an interpreter for students who are deaf or deaf-blind to communicate what exercise or activity is scheduled for the next station and/or the number of repetitions.
- An aide, volunteer, or peer tutor can assist the students who are deaf-blind to increase their understanding of the movement from station to station, activities, number of repetitions, and so forth.

INNOVATOR:
Candice Rehmeier
Nebraska School for the Visually Handicapped

GAME:	CATEGORY:
SOCKLEY	**ELEMENTARY/MIDDLE SCHOOL**

GOAL:
To improve fundamental motor patterns and skills, sport skills, agility, and CR and muscular endurance.

OBJECTIVE:
Students use a chosen manipulative skill to propel a ball or balloon.

EQUIPMENT:
- a balloon or punchball, or a ball on a string
- long, strong, smooth rope
- volleyball standards
- a small pulley or paper clip
- two flags

SETUP:
A long rope is placed across the gym and tied to hooks on each end of the wall or secured to two volleyball standards. The balloon, punchball, or ball on a string is suspended from the rope with either a pulley or large paper clip. This attachment allows the object to slide freely when hit. Flags are attached to the rope at an equal distance from the center for goal markers.

DESCRIPTION:
The students line up along the long string. Two teams are organized, with one, two, or three players on each team. Students in chairs can play against their ambulatory peers. The students hit the ball with the predetermined manipulative skill such as underhand hit, sidearm strike, or kick, and try to get it past the other team members and hit the flag. The ball may be raised or lowered to facilitate the chosen manipulative skill.

ADAPTATIONS:

■ Put bells in the balloon or punchball for students with some hearing.

■ Use this game as a lead-up game for soccer by lowering the ball so the students have to play with a kick. Lead up for volleyball by raising the ball high. Lead up for racquet skills by positioning the ball medium height.

■ Vary the distance of the students or the distance of the flags.

■ Change the roles of the students; encourage passing the ball.

■ Have a rule that students must use one hand, two hands, or only the dominant foot, and so on.

INNOVATOR:

Lauren Lieberman
SUNY Brockport

Adapted from the game of Sockley in:
Marsallo, M., Vacante, D. (1983). *Adapted Games and Motor Activities for Children.* Annandale, VA: Marsallo/Vacante.

GAME:	CATEGORY:
STEAL THE BACON	**ELEMENTARY/MIDDLE SCHOOL**

GOAL:
To improve fundamental motor patterns and skills, sport skills, agility, and balance.

OBJECTIVE:
Students play a team game utilizing their listening skills, locomotor skills, and speed.

EQUIPMENT
Mats, a bell, and a gym.

SETUP:
Place large mats end to end in the middle of the gym or room. Position members of each team a predetermined distance from the mats.

DESCRIPTION:
Assign each member of one team a number, animal, car, or like object. Do the same with the other team, so that players from each team have corresponding numbers or names. The instructor or volunteer stands in the middle of the mat with a bell. The instructor designates movement skills for students to use, then calls out a number(s), car(s), animal(s), or the like and rings the bell. The players with that number, car, animal, etc. move forward and attempt to touch the mat before their opponent does. The play continues until the teacher stops the competition.

ADAPTATIONS:
■ Match opposing players of similar ability.

■ Students can perform different locomotor skills to get to the mat: scoot, crawl, crab walk, jump, hop, skip, gallop, and so on.

■ Blindfold partially sighted students.

■ Play the game using carts, scooters, wheelchairs, or the like.

■ Provide assistance to those students who need interpreting, help to move, etc.

INNOVATOR:
Linda Gingery (retired)
Michigan School for the Blind

GAME:

T-BALL

CATEGORY:

ELEMENTARY/MIDDLE SCHOOL

GOAL:

To improve sport skills (baseball).

OBJECTIVE:

Students score points by hitting a ball off a T-stand and running the bases.

EQUIPMENT:

T-stand, Wiffle ball, and Wiffle bat.

SETUP:

Play on softball/baseball diamond with a T-stand on home plate. Blindfold partially sighted students. The playing field is divided into four areas, each representing either a single, double, triple or home run.

DESCRIPTION:

Each student adjusts the T-stand to the desired height, then assumes an appropriate batting stance. The student is allowed three swings to hit the ball. A single, double, triple or home run is earned if the student hits that ball in the corresponding area of the playing field. After hitting the ball, the student runs the designated number of bases to develop an awareness of the relationship of the four bases to the respective hit. A defensive player retrieves the ball and returns it to home plate for the next batter's turn. The batting and fielding teams change positions when all students have batted.

ADAPTATIONS:

■ Keep the number of students and teams small to allow for more participation.

■ Use a beeper ball for students who are blind.

■ Adjust the size of the softball or baseball diamond to fit the ability level of the students.

■ Use a time limit instead of a certain number of innings.

■ Call the batter out when a fielder stops a rolling audible ball or when the fielders perform some type of cooperative drill before the runner reaches the base. For example, after fielding the ball, the defending team might be required to form a line and pass the ball from one end to the other, alternating over the head with between the legs.

■ Assign a sighted person, such as a peer tutor, to run the bases with a student who is blind.

■ A staff member, volunteer, or peer tutor can assist students who are deaf-blind or have multiple disabilities to locate and place the ball on the T-stand, help the students swing the bat, locate a ball in the field, and so forth.

INNOVATOR:

John Schrock
Missouri School for the Blind

GAME:	CATEGORY:
TACTILE T-BALL (LEAD-UP GAME)	**MIDDLE SCHOOL**

GOAL:

To improve sport skills (baseball) and develop an understanding of the games of baseball and kickball.

OBJECTIVE:

Students hit a ball off a cone and run the bases independently.

EQUIPMENT:

Four tall cones, a long rope, a playground ball, and a bat.

SETUP:

Set up the cones in the shape of a baseball diamond. Wrap or tape rope around each cone in order to connect all the bases. Have two playing areas if sufficient staff or volunteers are available to help supervise.

DESCRIPTION:

Put the ball on the home plate cone. A student hits the ball off the cone (or hits a pitched ball), then runs around all the bases with or without trailing the rope. Have a different-textured surface on home plate so students who are blind know when they have reached home. Fielders retrieve the ball and return it to home plate. After batting, the student rotates to the field, and one of the fielders becomes a batter.

ADAPTATIONS:

■ Students with sight can be guide runners for students who are blind.

■ To make the guide rope easier to trail for taller students, raise the cones by placing them on a crate or box.

■ Use a beeper ball for students who are blind.

■ Use larger or smaller balls for different ability levels of students.

■ To accommodate individual student needs, use different types of bats, such as a flat bat, large pillow polo bat, or Wiffle ball bat.

■ Have an aide, volunteer, or peer tutor assist students who are deaf-blind or who have multiple disabilities to bat, run bases, or retrieve the ball.

INNOVATOR:

Monica Kleeman
Perkins School for the Blind

GAME:	CATEGORY:
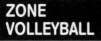 **ZONE VOLLEYBALL**	**ELEMENTARY/MIDDLE SCHOOL**

GOAL:

To improve sport skills (volleyball) and muscular endurance.

OBJECTIVE:

Students serve a volleyball from a predetermined distance into a designated area on the court.

EQUIPMENT:

Volleyball court, volleyball net, oversized trainer volleyballs, and floor marking tape.

SETUP:

Set up the volleyball net. Mark three or more serving areas as well as three serving lines (see diagram). The distance should reflect students' abilities.

DESCRIPTION:

In order to make the activity more of a game situation, points are assigned to designated areas of the court (refer to diagram). Students serve from behind any of the three serving lines. Once they select a serving line, five serves must be made from this area. In the next round they may select a different serving line. Games consist of as many rounds as the class period allows. Tournaments can be conducted and the standings carried over to the next day. Students may compete individually or as members of a team.

ADAPTATIONS:

■ Serving lines can be raised by taping cord to the floor.

■ Students can use either bright yellow oversized "trainer" volleyballs or regulation volleyballs (students select the size ball they want to use).

■ Voice or clapping can be used as directional prompts for students who are totally blind.

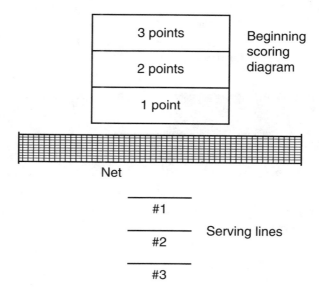

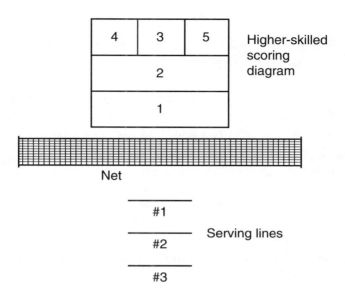

■ Various levels of assistance may be incorporated to teach students the serving motion. For example, students who are having difficulty executing the skill may be physically assisted through the task; or students able to perform the skill, yet limited in cognitive abilities, may be given a tactile signal (i.e., tap on the elbow to serve).

INNOVATOR:
Candice Rehmeier
Nebraska School for the Visually Handicapped

GAME:	CATEGORY:
ARCHERY BALLOON POP	**HIGH SCHOOL**

GOAL:
To improve sport skills (archery).

OBJECTIVE:
Students practice the basic shooting technique while attempting to pop balloons placed on an archery mat.

EQUIPMENT:
Archery bows, arrows, mats, ground quivers, balloons, mini beepers, footboards, and aiming devices.

SETUP:

Place balloons close together on the target mat. Have the shooting line 20-25 feet from the target.

DESCRIPTION:

While students practice their basic shooting technique, they attempt to break as many balloons as possible during their turn. The desire to break balloons seems to keep students focused on skill acquisition.

ADAPTATIONS:

■ Students having difficulty keeping an arrow on the arrow rest or string can use an arrow guide rest, arrow nocks (narrow enough for an arrow to snap onto the bow string), and finger guards (all items can be obtained from a local archery dealer or York Archery Supply, P.O. Box 110, Independence, MO 64051).

■ Students who are blind with hearing may benefit from the following devices:

1. A mini beeper placed on top of the archery mat for a directional cue. (Mini beeper can be obtained from Flaghouse, 150 N. MacQuesten Parkway, Mt. Vernon, NY 10550.)

2. A footboard [Hyman (1969) and Cowart (1993)]. Used to assist a student to assume a consistent body/foot position in relation to the target.

3. An aiming device [Taylor (1953), Reams (1980), Cowart (1993), and White (1995)]. Used by a student familiar with the basic shooting techniques to align an arrow with the target.

■ For students who are deaf-blind, the use of the footboard and aiming device have proven helpful in aligning themselves and the arrow to the target.

INNOVATOR:

Jim Cowart
California School for the Blind

GAME:	CATEGORY:
BEACH BALL VOLLEYBALL	**HIGH SCHOOL**

GOAL:
To improve sport skills (volleyball) and CR and muscular endurance.

OBJECTIVE:
Students volley a beach ball using adapted volleyball rules.

EQUIPMENT:
Volleyball or badminton net with standards, and a multi-colored beach ball.

SETUP:
Use a regular volleyball court.

DESCRIPTION:
The objective of the game is to see how long the students can keep a beach ball in the air. (Students or staff can keep track of the number of hits or the length of time the two teams are able to continually volley the ball.) The slower flight of the beach ball allows the students with physical disabilities more time to get in position to play the ball. The serve can be a punch, hit, or throw; assistance can be given by other players to get the ball over the net.

ADAPTATIONS:
■ Beach balls of different sizes can be used according to the ability or age of the students.

■ Add a teaspoon of uncooked rice to the inside of the beach ball to allow for auditory tracking.

■ Use hand clapping or verbal prompts as directional cues for students who are blind.

■ Tie the beach ball to the net with long string so students do not have to chase it.

■ To make it possible for students limited in movement to successfully participate, use a large balloon; reduce court size; permit one or two bounces; allow students to catch the ball or move closer to the net; permit an unlimited number of hits or people touching the ball; and so on.

INNOVATORS:
Karen Allen and Stephen Kearney
Oklahoma School for the Blind

GAME: CATEGORY:

BEEP   **HIGH**
BASEBALL ·   **SCHOOL**

GOAL:
    To improve sport skills (baseball).

OBJECTIVE:
    The batter must reach a buzzing base before a fielder has possession of
    the ball.

EQUIPMENT:
    A 16-inch softball containing an auditory beeper; two bases that are 48-
    inch vertical pylons in which electronic devices emit a buzzing sound
    when activated. (Bases are 90 feet down their respective lines, and 5 feet
    off the foul line.)

SETUP:
    See diagram.

DESCRIPTION:
    A team is made up of six players who are blind or visually impaired, and
    two sighted individuals. The sighted participants play pitcher and

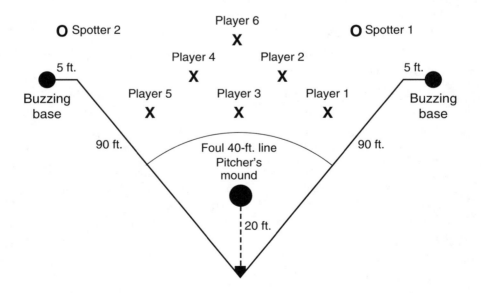

catcher on offense, and spotters on defense. Players bat on offense, and field on defense. The pitcher tries to hit the bat of the batter with the ball. The batter tries to swing the bat through the same arc each time. A well-hit ball is the cooperative effort of the pitcher and the batter. When the ball is hit, the batter runs to either first or third base, depending upon which base the umpire activates. A run is scored when the batter reaches first or third base before a defender holds the ball off the ground. If a defender picks up the ball before the base runner reaches the base, the base runner is out.

SELECTED GAME RULES:

Taken from information provided by the National Beep Baseball Association: Jeanette Bigger, 2231 West 1st Ave., Topeka, KS 66606-1304, (913) 276-0345-work (913) 234-2156-home

■ Games are six innings in length.

■ Players with a visual classification of light perception or better must wear blindfolds.

■ A minimum of one but not more than two spotters assist the defensive team. They vocally assist the defense in positioning themselves on the field of play before the ball is struck. They also may advise if a batter is right-handed or left-handed and provide other data they feel their players should know. Once a ball is struck, a spotter may call out only the name or number of the person in the best position to field the ball.

■ A batter swinging at a pitched ball is allowed five strikes before being called out. Foul balls are considered strikes, but the fifth strike must be a clear miss.

■ A batter may allow two balls to go by without penalty. Any additional balls not swung at will be called strikes by the umpire.

■ Each team is allowed three outs per time at bat.

■ An out is recorded either by a strike-out or by a struck fair ball being cleanly fielded by a defensive player prior to the runner's reaching the buzzing base. The defensive player must have definite in-hand and off-the-ground possession of the ball in the opinion of the umpire.

■ The pitcher must have one foot in contact with the pitching mark (which is 20 feet from home plate) when delivering the ball.

■ The pitcher is obligated to give two verbal alerts to the batter. The first, "Ready," must be clearly audible to defense players. This means the pitcher is about to deliver the ball. The second, "Pitch" or "Ball," must also be audible to the defense players and must be said as the ball is being released.

ADAPTATIONS:

■ Students having trouble locating the base may be provided a sighted guide, or the base may be moved closer.

■ Students having difficulty locating the ball may be given verbal prompts as needed and/or provided physical assistance.

■ Students unable to hit a pitched ball may use a batting tee and/or be provided physical assistance.

INNOVATOR:

Contributed by Jim Cowart
California School for the Blind

GAME:	CATEGORY:
 **FRISBEE BELL HOCKEY**	**MIDDLE/HIGH SCHOOL**

GOAL:

To improve sport skills (hockey), agility, balance, and cardiorespiratory and muscular endurance.

OBJECTIVE:

Students play hockey using a bright Frisbee with bells for tracking.

EQUIPMENT:

Frisbees, bells, string, enough hockey sticks for each student, and cones or hockey goals.

SETUP:

Tie strings across the bottom of the Frisbee from one side to the other with three to five bells attached to the string evenly across the bottom. Because the Frisbee is brighter and slower moving and forms a larger target to hit, it serves well as the puck or ball in a hockey game for students with visual impairments.

DESCRIPTION:

Divide the class evenly. Have one team in red pinnies and one in blue (or shirts and skins, white and dark—whatever helps distinguish teams). Play the game of indoor hockey using the Frisbee with bells. The Frisbee promotes increased success and elevates the level of excitement in a game.

ADAPTATIONS:

■ Use lead-up activities such as "dribbling" the Frisbee around cones under control, hitting the Frisbee back and forth with a friend, or shooting the goal from different angles and distances.

■ For students in wheelchairs, the grip on the hockey stick may have to be modified, or the time given to hit the Frisbee may need to be increased. You may also make a rule that a particular student must hit the Frisbee before that team can score.

■ A guide or peer tutor may be needed for students with less vision.

■ The use of flags and signs can aid in communication for students who are deaf.

■ Use a beep baseball as the puck.

INNOVATOR:

Lauren Lieberman
SUNY Brockport

GAME:	CATEGORY:
FRISBEE GOLF	**MIDDLE/HIGH SCHOOL**

GOAL:
To improve sport skills (Frisbee) and CR endurance.

OBJECTIVE:
Students throw the Frisbee at the flag and try to get it inside the hula hoop around the flag in the least amount of throws.

EQUIPMENT:
Three to nine bicycle flags (large orange flags), three to nine hula hoops, one Frisbee for each student, and one card for each student with a pen to keep score.

SETUP:
In a field or big grassy setting, set the bike flags inside the hula hoop. Space flags 4-20 feet from each other depending upon the throwing ability of the students.

DESCRIPTION:
Students start at flag #1. From there they try to throw the Frisbee to the #2 flag and land the Frisbee in the hula hoop around the flag. Students try to accomplish this goal with the least amount of throws possible. Students add up how many throws it takes to complete the course, as in the game of golf. The course may be set up with 3 flags all the way up to 9 or 18 flags depending upon class time and student ability. Students with limited vision and/or hearing may need staff or peer help with the direction of the flag. (They can use pointing and/or a clapper.) When the students get closer to the hula hoop, they can feel the hoop and then walk to their Frisbee to understand the distance between the two.

ADAPTATIONS:
■ Students with low vision may prefer a particular color Frisbee in order to see the contrast against the grass or gym floor.

■ Students may want to compete only against themselves, or against other students. At the end of the unit, the staff can compete against the students (blindfolded)!

■ If the space is limited, or if only an indoor area is available, set up the same formation with cones in the middle of the hoops.

■ Students with a limited range of motion or limited gripping ability may have flags set closer together, or they may be allowed to start 2-3 feet from each flag.

■ If your school or program is limited in funds, write to your local Domino's Pizza, and they usually will send big, bright Frisbees for free! Another source of information related to Frisbees is Wham-O, Inc., Sports Promotion Department, 835 E. El Monte Street, San Gabriel, CA 91778.

INNOVATOR:
Lauren Lieberman
SUNY Brockport

GAME:	CATEGORY:
HOME RUN DERBY	**HIGH SCHOOL**

GOAL:
To improve sport skills (baseball).

OBJECTIVE:
Students play a modified game of baseball. The game is individually adapted to meet the needs of each player.

EQUIPMENT:
A softball-sized Wiffle ball—color should contrast with the batting tee and gym walls and floors, an adjustable batting tee or pylons that can be stacked to adjust height, and four rubber bases whose color contrasts with the floor.

SETUP:
Set up the gym with four bases in a diamond shape. Mark scoring areas with colored tape.

DESCRIPTION:
Teams consist of four to five players. With teams of this size, the positions are limited to a pitcher and three or four fielders. Each player bats every inning; after all have batted, the teams switch positions. Depending on the batting ability of the students, they can receive a pitched ball or hit the ball off a batting tee. The following game rules apply: Singles, doubles, triples, and home runs are determined by the ball landing in designated areas clearly marked with colored tape. For example, singles are balls hit in the infield, doubles are balls hit in the outfield, triples are balls hit below the 15-foot line on the wall, and home runs are balls hit on or above the 15-foot line. The designated areas can be modified for gym size, ceiling height, and so forth. A student runs to the base that corresponds to his or her hit (e.g., a student who hits a double runs to second base). The base runner advances according to the hit by the following runner. Runs are scored either by advancing a runner to home plate or by hitting a home run. Imaginary base runners can be used if needed instead of allowing the students to run the bases.

ADAPTATIONS:
■ Play "Drawball," in which students draw a card out of a box that tells if their hit is a single, double, triple, or home run. Students advance

bases accordingly. The teams change from offense to defense after all players have had a turn drawing a card.

■ Use a brighter, slower, or auditory ball to aid in success.

■ Use different sizes of bats depending upon the need.

■ Staff, volunteers, or peers can assist students who need help to bat, field, or run bases.

■ Students with visual impairments may need a sighted guide or a guide wire when running bases.

■ Students in wheelchairs or using crutches may need additional physical assistance.

INNOVATORS:
Stephen Kearney and Karen Allen
Oklahoma School for the Blind

GAME:	CATEGORY:
GOAL BALL	**MIDDLE/HIGH SCHOOL**

GOAL:
To improve sport skills (goal ball), agility, CR endurance, flexibility, and muscular endurance and strength.

OBJECTIVE:
Students try to roll the goal ball over the goal line of their opponents.

EQUIPMENT:
Goal ball (purchased through the American Foundation for the Blind, 1-800-AFBLIND), knee and elbow pads (sporting goods stores, Kmart), blindfolds (Pro Optics, 317 Woodwork Lane, Palatine, IL 60057), nonstretch rope or cord (any hardware store), and 3-inch-wide tape (3M packing tape is preferable). Be sure tape does not mark the gym floor.

SETUP:
Mark out playing area as shown in the diagram with cord held to the floor by tape.

DESCRIPTION:
The teams may consist of up to six players, with no more than three players per team on the court at the same time. Substitution may be made during any stoppage of play. Each player must wear a blindfold

during the course of the game. The referee (teacher) should prohibit all crowd noise, especially coaching from the crowd. The team starting with the ball (offense) rolls the goal ball on the ground at the other team with the intention of scoring. Scoring occurs when the goal ball crosses the goal line or back line in the court. The team receiving the ball (defense) tries to stop the ball by diving in front of it and gaining possession of the ball without the other team scoring. That team then becomes the offensive team. Each team has a center (the player playing in front and middle) and two wings, playing one to the right of center and one to the left, 2-3 feet behind the position of the center.

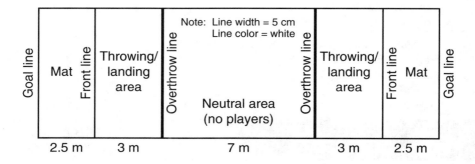

PENALTIES:

■ No player may defend the ball in front of the "front line" of their playing area.

■ Players may not use vision in any way as part of the game.

■ Once possession of the ball is obtained, the offensive team has 8 seconds to roll the ball.

■ No player may roll the ball more than two consecutive times for his or her team.

■ Any balls rolled by the offensive team must contact the ground at least once before crossing the "overthrow line."

PENALTY SHOT:

When a penalty shot is awarded, the player who caused the penalty remains on the court while his or her teammates leave the court. The penalized player has to single-handedly defend against a penalty throw. Any player who is on the offensive team at the time of the infraction may take the penalty throw. Following the penalty throw, play stops while the removed players return to the court.

ADAPTATIONS:

■ For students who lack hearing as well as vision, use a peer or teacher to tap their shoulder to indicate ball position—soft and to the right for a ball that is close to them on the right, soft and left for a ball that is close to them on the left, harder and to the right for a ball for which they need to dive to the right, and harder to the left for a ball arriving farther to the left.

■ Students with limited lower-body control start in a kneeling or sitting position.

■ Use a task-analysis approach for students unable to throw or catch the goal ball.

More information about Goal Ball, the rules, training camps, and tournaments can be obtained from the United States Association for Blind Athletes (USABA) National Office in Colorado Springs, CO 80903, 719-630-0422; or from USABA Goal Ball Chairman Stephen Kearney, Box 309, Muskogee, OK 74401, 918-682-6641.

INNOVATOR:

Lauren Lieberman
SUNY Brockport
(taken in part from the Maine Goal Ball Team's "The Maine Squeeze" Goal Ball Rules)

GAME:	CATEGORY:
MODERN DANCE	**HIGH SCHOOL**

GOAL:

To improve agility, flexibility, balance, cardiovascular and muscular endurance, and fundamental motor patterns and skills.

OBJECTIVE:

Students perform a dance consisting of familiar moves and music.

EQUIPMENT:

A large open space and music. Modern funky music tends to motivate the students most.

SETUP:

Students start in a line or circle formation with arms on each other's shoulders or holding hands. The teacher first explains the moves, then adds music.

DESCRIPTION:

Students stand in a line and wait for the teacher's command. The teacher makes moves related to a one-word command. For example, "Circles" means to make arm circles; "Bend" indicates side bends; "Knees"means to march in place; "Up-back" indicates walking forward for eight counts and back for eight counts; "Hips" means to sway the hips. Each move is performed for one or two sets of eight counts. The moves can be as simple or complex as necessary. The goal to keep in mind is student success. Formation can vary from a line, to a circle, to a "U" shape, or in partners. Strive for repetitious movements within each student's capability. When the class has learned five or six moves in a row, put those moves to music, and repeat the sequence. The results will be sensational! Extra teachers, volunteers, and peer tutors will help make the dance successful.

ADAPTATIONS:

■ Students with limited mobility or students with hearing impairments can be placed next to a volunteer, teacher, or peer tutor for the appropriate cue. The students with hearing impairments may need a tactile cue.

■ After a 6-to-8-week unit, students may elect to perform a dance show!

■ Allow the students to form the dance moves using their imaginations.

INNOVATOR:

Lauren Lieberman
SUNY Brockport

GAME:	CATEGORY:
AUDITORY BOWLING	**RECREATION**

GOAL:

To improve sport and recreation skills (bowling).

OBJECTIVE:

Participants move milk jugs by striking them with a rolling ball. They then determine what substance is in the jug.

EQUIPMENT:

Three to five milk jugs, dirt, rice, water, bells, macaroni, tape, and an 8-inch playground ball.

SETUP:

Line up three to five milk jugs (depending upon the ability level of the student) 1-2 feet in front of a 4-foot line, as shown in the diagram.

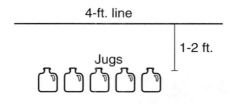

4-ft. line

Jugs

1-2 ft.

O Students (sit or stand)

DESCRIPTION:

Put a different substance in each jug (e.g., one with 10 bells, one with 1 cup of rice, one with 2 cups of water, one with 3 cups of dirt, etc.), enough to make a distinct sound when the jug is hit with a ball. Be sure that the lids are closed tightly on each jug. Then line the participants up 6-10 feet in front of the jugs, depending upon their ability. Have the participants roll the ball at the jugs and see if they can hit the jug over the 4-foot line for 5 points, then determine what substance is in the jug for another 5 points. Each participant gets two or three turns per round, playing five to seven rounds. The participants who are able can keep score for themselves.

ADAPTATIONS:

■ Use painted jugs for students who have low vision and little hearing.

■ Mark letters or numbers on the front of jugs. After the jug is hit over the 4-foot line, participants can identify the letters or numbers for double points.

■ Participants in chairs can roll the ball down a large tube or a ramp.

■ Use more jugs for participants who need a larger range and fewer jugs for participants who need a smaller range.

■ Have a higher functioning participant set up the jugs.

■ Use a heavier ball for participants who need more sensory feedback.

INNOVATOR:

Lauren Lieberman

SUNY Brockport

GAME:	CATEGORY:
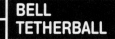 **BELL TETHERBALL**	**RECREATION**

GOAL:

To improve fundamental motor patterns and skills.

OBJECTIVE:

Participants use tetherball skills to wrap the ball and string around the tetherball pole.

EQUIPMENT:

A soft ball such as a punchball, beach ball, balloon, or Sensory Oriented Ball or Balzac Ball (a ball made out of fabric stuffed with stockings or styrofoam peanuts) all having some type of auditory element such as bells, rice, or popcorn kernels inside; string or cord; and a volleyball standard or tetherball standard.

SETUP:

Tie string or cord to the standard and to the ball at the appropriate height. Secure the ball approximately a foot above the participant's head if trying to promote the overhead throw, shoulder height for encouraging sidearm motion, waist level for the underhand throw, and on the ground to promote kicking.

DESCRIPTION:

After organizing the game for the desired skill, set up the standard with one participant on each side. Tell each participant to hit the ball past the opponent using the appropriate skill. The "round" is over when the string and ball are wrapped all the way around the pole. Additional rounds can be played as time allows.

ADAPTATIONS:

■ Participants in chairs can play with ambulatory participants; however, they may need rule modifications (e.g., no more than two hits in a row, no smashing the ball, etc.).

■ Softer balls may be used for participants who are tactile-defensive or are afraid of harder balls.

■ Allow participants to choose the height of the ball and the skill.

■ Participants who need more skill development may practice without competition. For example, give the command, "Hit the ball overhead until it is totally wrapped around the pole." This approach allows the participants to be independent while working on a skill at the same time.

INNOVATOR:

Lauren Lieberman
SUNY Brockport

GAME:	CATEGORY:
BOWLING PIN POSITION	**RECREATION**

GOAL:
> To improve sport skills (bowling).

OBJECTIVE:
> Participants deliver a bowling ball. The teacher alerts participants to the number of standing pins; in turn, the participants relate the position/ location of the standing pins.

EQUIPMENT:
> Bowling guide rail, bowling ball (6 pounds and heavier), bowling pins, and a magnetic pin position board.

SETUP:
> Set up equipment at a community bowling establishment or school gym.

DESCRIPTION:
> While practicing a method for consistently delivering a bowling ball toward the pins, the participant is becoming aware of pin position. Once the delivery begins to become consistent, the participant is ready to learn how to convert spares. Initially, the instructor uses a magnetic pin position board to assist visually impaired participants in learning bowling pin numbers as well as their position on the pin deck. Through feeling and with verbal input from the instructor, most higher function- ing participants learn quickly. Once the participant is aware of pin numbers and position, the instructor tells the participant the numbers of the pins left standing after the participant's first and/or second delivery of the ball. In turn, the participant tells the teacher the position and location of the standing pins. For example, the participant is told pins 6, 7, and 10 remain standing after delivery; in turn, the participant tells the instructor that #7 is on the left side of the pin deck, and #6 and #10 are on the right side. Participants enjoy the challenge of stating pin position without making an error.

ADAPTATIONS:
> ■ Participants who are blind or deaf-blind may benefit from the following options:
>
> 1. A bowling guide rail. This is used to direct the participant from the beginning of an approach to the foul line.

2. A magnetic pin position board. Ten small magnets are placed on a metal base (4 inches by 4 inches) as they are positioned on the pin deck. The top of each magnet and its position on the metal base is brailled with the numbers 1-10. Magnets can be easily removed by the teacher to represent a pin or pins knocked down. By feel, a participant can easily determine the numbers of the pins knocked down as well as the location of standing pins.

3. A gutter guard can be used to ensure no balls go in the gutter, thereby increasing success.

■ Participants with limited mobility can sit on a chair at the foul line to deliver the bowling ball.

INNOVATOR:

Jim Cowart

California School for the Blind

GAME:	CATEGORY:
FITNESS WHEEL	**RECREATION**

GOAL:

To improve flexibility, strength, muscular and CR endurance, and fundamental motor patterns and skills.

OBJECTIVE:

Participants spin the fitness wheel, identify the area to which the dial is pointing, and perform the assigned task.

EQUIPMENT:

A spin dial (homemade or from an old board game) and three or more objects to place on the dial as needed.

SETUP:

Make a dial with different exercises printed on it such as skipping, galloping, jumping jacks, sit-ups, push-ups, running laps, etc. The skills and exercises should also be printed in braille. This dial or an additional dial can also be made with pictures of the activity as well as words to give the participants more information. For participants who are deaf-blind, a dial can be made with shapes and objects to represent exercises, such as a soft piece of fabric (representing a mat) for push-ups and sit-ups; a small card for running laps; a balloon for skipping and galloping; and a piece of Velcro for jumping jacks, etc.

DESCRIPTION:

This game can be played in a group or by an individual. Points can be accumulated for identification, for the performance of a skill, or both. A participant spins the dial. When the dial stops, the participant must identify (by either the word or object) the exercise to be performed in that area. Identification of the correct exercise can earn the participant a point. The participant then performs the skill. Participants who perform the skill correctly get one point. Each person gets a turn. The person or team with the most points wins.

ADAPTATIONS:

■ Give each participant a dial adapted to his or her ability level.

■ Use different activities for different units, such as different types of throws with a throwing unit, different gymnastics moves for a gymnastics unit, different locomotor skills for a locomotor skills unit, etc.

■ Use the same approach with aquatics skills (or locomotor skills) in the pool.

■ If the group includes participants with physical limitations, add skills to the fitness wheel for them. Skills should be challenging but attainable for all participants.

INNOVATOR:

Beth Hudy
Royer Greaves School for the Blind

GAME:	CATEGORY:
GOLDEN SNEAKER CLUB	**RECREATION**

GOAL:

To improve CR and muscular endurance and sport skills (track).

OBJECTIVE:

Participants are given two class periods a week in order to walk and/or run at their own pace on the track and/or cross-country course. Participants record the distance walked/run on a large chart; the objective is to reach 25 miles in order to earn a "Golden Sneaker" trophy.

EQUIPMENT

Chart for recording miles walked/run.

SETUP:

Track or any area where distance can be accurately marked.

DESCRIPTION:

This is an activity that is self-motivating. Participants walk/run using guide wires or sighted guides. They have the option to walk/run either the track or cross-country course during the time provided to give some variety. (The cross-country course can be designed by the participants.) Participants' progress is recorded on a large chart. At the end of the term, every participant who has accumulated 25 miles or more is awarded a "Golden Sneaker" trophy at a special assembly. The trophies can be actual tennis shoes glued to wooden bases and sprayed with gold paint. Lettering on the plaques indicates the participant's name and number of miles walked/run.

ADAPTATIONS:

■ Names on trophies can be brailled or noted in large print.

■ Students can record their progress on a computer.

■ For students with limited mobility, require fewer miles walked or wheeled in order to achieve an award.

INNOVATOR:

Candace Rehmeier
Nebraska School for the Visually Handicapped

GAME:	CATEGORY:
HOLIDAY ROLLER SKATING	**RECREATION**

GOAL:

To improve balance, agility, CR endurance, and sport skills (roller skating).

OBJECTIVE

Participants roller-skate independently and purposefully around the gym.

EQUIPMENT:

Four cones, roller skates, Nyloop target, cut-out felt shapes (objects or shapes vary depending on the holiday theme), and Velcro.

SETUP:

Participants can be motivated by using a thematic approach to the lesson.

DESCRIPTION:

Participants roller-skate around once and pick up a heart. The next time around they place the heart on the Nyloop target. Repeat as many times

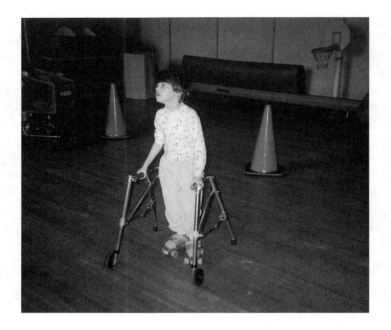

EXAMPLE: VALENTINE'S DAY

Place cones around the gym in a circle (connect them with rope if necessary). At one end of the gym place the Nyloop target on the wall. Next to the target place all the cut-out hearts on a table (put a small piece of Velcro on the back of each heart).

as possible in the time allowed. Challenge the participants to add one more lap each session.

ADAPTATIONS:

■ Change the object or shape according to the new theme: ornaments on a Christmas tree, Easter eggs in a basket, candles on a menorah, stars on a flag, pumpkins on the ground, apples in a tree, and so on.

■ If you do not have Nyloop, or felt squares, cut out objects or shapes from paper and place tape on one side. Participants can stick them on the gym wall.

■ Have races around the gym or up and back for relays.

■ Give each participant different numbers of laps and objects or shapes according to their ability.

- Set up a smaller circular rink for participants with limited mobility.

- This same concept can be used for locomotor skills, walking, running, and swimming laps.

INNOVATOR:

Monica Kleeman

Perkins School for the Blind

GAME:	CATEGORY:
SCATTER STATIONS	**RECREATION**

GOAL:

To improve agility, balance, flexibility, strength, muscular and CR endurance, and fundamental motor patterns and skills.

OBJECTIVE:

Students read or listen to directions and perform various movements and exercises.

EQUIPMENT:

Laminated cards with directions in large print, braille, and/or pictures; and bells or other sound cues.

SETUP:

Place the exercise/activity cards at stations around the room or gym.

DESCRIPTION:

The leader begins the activity by reading the designated motor skill and specific exercises noted on station #1's card. This is followed by activating a sound cue at station #1. On hearing the sound, all participants move to the first station by performing the designated motor skill (e.g., walk, crawl, roll, spin etc.). Once participants locate station #1's card and leader, they execute the specific exercise. After the exercise is completed, another participant reads the movement and exercise for station #2. A sound device is activated for station #2, and all students move to that station using the specific motor skill and perform the noted exercise. This continues until all the cards have been read at least once. Exercise ideas include 10 side leg raises, 10 push-ups, 10 bent knee sit-ups, 10 jumping jacks, 10 arm circles, 10 deep breaths, 10 alternate toe touches, 10 trunk extensions, etc.

ADAPTATIONS:

■ Use equipment such as mats, balls, beanbags, hoops, and jump ropes.

■ Additional activity ideas include balancing a beanbag on the head, tossing a beanbag and catching it, doing a forward roll, dribbling 10 times in a row, jumping rope three times without missing, standing on one foot, and twirling the hula hoop for a count of five.

■ Participants who are blind may be paired with a peer tutor.

■ Vary activities according to the functional level of participants and the goal of the activity.

■ Participants can choose to return to an activity after they have completed all stations.

■ If there are participants in the group with limited physical abilities, include activities on the cards for them as well. For example, participants in chairs may do arm circles when the other participants are performing jumping jacks, or they can perform wheelchair push-ups while the other participants are performing regular push-ups.

INNOVATOR:

Linda Webbert
Maryland School for the Blind

GAME:	CATEGORY:
SENSATIONAL PING-PONG	**RECREATION**

GOAL:

To improve sport skills (Ping-Pong), flexibility, and muscular endurance.

OBJECTIVE:

Participants stand or sit at a Ping-Pong table and hit a balloon back and forth over the net.

EQUIPMENT:

Ping-Pong paddles, balloons, Ping-Pong table, string, and bells (optional).

SETUP:

One or two players play on each side of the table.

DESCRIPTION:

Participants play a regular game of Ping-Pong using a balloon. The balloon should be a color that contrasts well with the table and adjacent walls. If the students need more auditory prompts, bells can be put inside

the balloon. Regular Ping-Pong rules can be used, or students may count the number of consecutive times they hit the balloon over the net.

ADAPTATIONS:

■ Students with less muscular control can hit the balloon with a paddle having a larger head, or with their hand.

■ Using a string, tie the balloon to the net so students do not need to chase it all around.

■ Participants who are higher functioning can use a small beach ball or a small Nerf ball (or a regular Ping-Pong ball if possible).

INNOVATOR:

Lauren Lieberman
SUNY Brockport

GAME:	CATEGORY:
SHOWDOWN	**RECREATION**

GOAL:

To improve sport skills (showdown).

OBJECTIVE:

A player hits the ball under the center bar and into the opponent's goal.

EQUIPMENT:

■ A hollow toy plastic baseball (approximately 2-3/4 inches in diameter) containing 5-7 beebees.

■ A bat—similar to a small cricket bat (the blade is approximately 3 inches by 10 inches and is attached to a 5-inch handle).

■ A table, consisting of a flat playing surface (approximately 4 feet by 12 feet), ringed by a 5-inch frame. Each table corner features a quarter-circle. A small goal box (6 inches by 3 inches) is located at each end of the table.

■ A T-bar with a panel which splits the table and rests on the side frames (the panel prevents sighted players from anticipating shots from blind opponents).

DESCRIPTION:

One player begins play by placing the ball in front of his or her bat and hitting it toward the opponent's goal. The served ball must hit the side wall prior to passing under the center divider. The defender waits for the served ball with his or her bat on the table in front of the goal, with the blade slanted slightly forward (to direct the ball to the table surface). On returning the ball, the defender may use a push shot (pushing the ball), wrist shot (flicking the wrist), slap shot (hitting the ball from a few inches back), handle shot (the ball hits the handle), and so forth. Following the return, the player again places the bat in front of the goal in preparation to block and return the next shot. Play continues until a point is scored or the game is won by one of the players.

SELECTED GAME RULES:

Taken from "Showdown Coaching Manual, Level 1"

■ The game is played with two or four players.

■ The first team to reach 11 points and be ahead by a minimum of 2 points wins the game.

■ A match consists of the best two out of three games.

■ The player who begins the game serves five times consecutively, then relinquishes service to the opponent.

■ The ball must pass under the center divider to be considered in play.

■ The bat must be held in only one hand.

■ Scoring: Two points are awarded for a goal. In addition, your opponent gets a point if any of the following occur: the ball is hit off your side of the table, the ball hits the screen, or the ball is touched with any part of your body other than the bat or batting hand up to and including your wrist.

ADAPTATIONS:

■ Participants having difficulty tracking the ball may be provided verbal prompts and/or physical assistance.

■ Participants having trouble hitting the ball may be given physical assistance based on level of need.

■ Participants who are deaf with some sight can use their vision to play the game.

For further information and complete rules, write: Canadian Blind Sports Association, 333 River Road, Ottowa, ON KIL 8H9.

INNOVATOR:

Contributed by Jim Cowart
California School for the Blind

GAME:	CATEGORY:
SUCCESS-ORIENTED HORSESHOES	**RECREATION**

GOAL:

To improve sport skills (horseshoes) and muscular strength.

OBJECTIVE:

Participants play the game of horseshoes and experience success no matter what the physical limitation. (This game promotes success because more stakes are used and because the stakes are longer and thicker, so the student is more likely to hit the stake or get a ringer!)

EQUIPMENT:

20 stakes 2 feet long and at least 1 inch thick (ask the woodworking teacher, or buy inexpensive ones at a hardware store) and 6-10 plastic horseshoes.

SETUP:

Set up the stakes outside in the grass, in an arrangement that will promote success for the participants. For participants with less ability, set up several stakes and place them one horseshoe width apart. For participants with a higher ability, set up fewer stakes, farther apart. If the class includes participants of various abilities, set all the stakes close together, and have the more experienced participants stand farther back. Use either of the stake formations noted below in the diagram. Also change the setup so participants have to vary their shots.

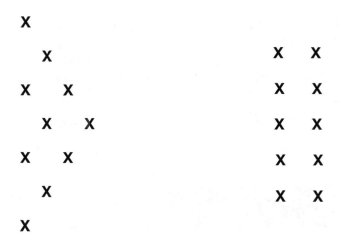

DESCRIPTION:

Participants play a game of horseshoes with two to four horseshoes each. Scoring could be 5 points if the horseshoe is touching the stake, 10 points if it is leaning on the stake, and 20 points for a ringer. Allow participants to keep their own scores when possible. Participants in chairs may throw from closer distances such as 2-10 feet away. Participants who are totally blind may walk the distance of the course, feel the formation of the stakes, and have a peer guide to point them in the right direction when throwing.

ADAPTATIONS:

■ Tap the stakes for a directional cue for participants who are totally blind.

■ Have tournaments against classmates and staff.

■ Play indoors with small, thin cones, or stakes that screw into a wooden stand.

■ Use larger horseshoes for even more success!

■ Color-code the stakes for more complicated scoring. Also make scoring areas in the grass surrounding the stakes so participants have a better chance to get points with every throw.

INNOVATOR:
Lauren Lieberman
SUNY Brockport

GAME:	CATEGORY:
TACTILE TWISTER	**RECREATION**

GOAL:
To improve flexibility, muscular strength, balance, and muscular endurance.

OBJECTIVE:
Participants play the game of Twister with tactile cues.

EQUIPMENT:
One large bedsheet (preferably full, queen, or king size), glue, glitter, cut-out shapes (preferably familiar shapes), and an 8 inch by 8 inch piece of cardboard for the spinner.

SETUP:
Trace the shapes with a pencil in rows onto the sheet. Cover the traced outline of the shapes with glue, then cover the glue with glitter. Use a different color of glitter for each shape. Spread the sheet out, and secure the corners with a cone, Velcro, or a staff person. Two to five participants can play at the same time while one student serves as the spinner. The spinner can be made by cutting an arrow out of cardboard and securing it to the middle of the spinner board with a long pushpin or tack. (Be sure to protect the back with cork or tape.) Draw a vertical line and a horizontal line through the middle of the spinner board to separate the board into quadrants. Draw a body part in each quadrant: left hand in top left quadrant, right hand in top right quadrant, left foot in bottom left quadrant, and right foot in bottom right quadrant. Then draw all four

shapes in each quadrant. If the spinner stops on the top right quadrant, the call would be "right hand" and the name of the shape in which the arrow is pointing. Braille the name of the shapes and body parts under each one for children who are blind.

DESCRIPTION:

The student who is the spinner spins the dial and calls out the commands. For example, "Right foot on the square, and left hand on the triangle" or "Left foot on the star, and right hand on the circle." Allow the participants to continue for a set number of spins or for a set time.

ADAPTATIONS:

■ Instead of using glitter, the instructor may sew different shapes of various colors, textures, and materials onto the sheet in rows. Material such as corduroy, silk, velvet, or polyester can be used.

■ Braille the spinner for participants who are blind.

■ Sign commands to participants who are hard of hearing or deaf.

■ Use physical guidance for participants who have limited tactile ability.

■ Participants who are very physically disabled can play in their chairs. Make a special Tactile Twister sheet for them, and hang it over a table or chair. Make all the shapes closer together and in one place, so that participants with limited range of motion can touch all the shapes from their chairs.

■ The instructor can also be the spinner for participants who cannot spin for themselves.

INNOVATOR:
Lauren Lieberman
SUNY Brockport

GAME:	CATEGORY:
TEAM CONE CROQUET	**RECREATION (ALL AGES)**

GOAL:
To improve sport skills (croquet).

OBJECTIVE:
Participants learn croquet skills as well as team play.

EQUIPMENT:
A croquet set, large orange cone markers, and broken hula hoops.

SETUP:
The game is set up almost like the game of croquet, except large orange cone field markers are used instead of arches. The two ends of the broken hula hoops are placed in the top of each pair of cone markers.

DESCRIPTION:
Participants work as a team and must alternate hits. They start at an end stake and hit the croquet ball toward two cones set up side by side with a small space between them. Blind participants may use the side of the mallet instead of the end, providing a larger area with which to hit. Partners may tap on the cones or clap to direct the hits for blind participants. Participants may also want to feel the ball, then walk to the cone to understand the distance between the two. There can be as many as four participants on a team, utilizing one croquet mallet and ball per team. The teams as well as players within the teams take turns. Regular croquet rules apply if another person's ball is hit. Arrange the cones in

any pattern that you wish. The setup can be simplified to reduce playing time. The first team to get back to the end stake (or cone) is the winner. Other options include competition or the use of scorecards to note the number of hits it takes to complete the course.

ADAPTATIONS:

■ Use large orange field marker cones.

■ It may help to spray the croquet balls a brighter color.

■ A larger ball such as a playground ball or volleyball may be used to increase success.

■ Participants who are blind or deaf-blind may need sign or verbal cues directing them to their ball or the opponent's ball.

■ Participants with limited physical ability may need assistance holding onto the mallet, hitting the ball, or ambulating. These adjustments can be incorporated into the rules.

INNOVATOR:

Candice Rehmeier
Nebraska School for the Visually Handicapped

GAME:

CATEGORY:

BODY PAINTING

AQUATICS (ALL AGES)

GOAL:

To increase water adjustment and flexibility.

OBJECTIVE:

Students practice total body washing/showering.

EQUIPMENT:

Body paints (water-based paint), paintbrushes, washcloths, and soap.

SETUP:

Locker room or shower. Students and staff wear swimsuits.

DESCRIPTION:

Individuals body-paint themselves and/or each other using water-based paints in bright colors. Use terms such as, "Can you paint your knee?" "Can you make your elbow red?" "Paint your partner's feet blue!" and so on. After painting, students shower, being sure to wash or scrub to remove all the paint.

ADAPTATIONS:

■ Direct the activity to include specific identification of body parts— for example, paint legs, wash legs.

■ Direct the activity to include color identification— red on the right leg, blue on the left, and so on.

■ Students with low vision or no vision may want to use a specific textured paint.

INNOVATOR:

Sue Grosse
Milwaukee High School of the Arts

GAME:

CATEGORY:

BUCKET PLAY

AQUATICS (ELEMENTARY)

GOAL:

To improve water adjustment and flexibility.

OBJECTIVE:

Students perform a variety of motor tasks that require handling and manipulating objects in the water.

EQUIPMENT:

Buckets, pails, tubs, scoops, poker chips, cups, sponges.

SETUP:

Locker room, room with drain in floor, outdoor grass or solid surface, or shallow children's wading pool. Individuals should wear swim attire.

DESCRIPTION:

Individuals manipulate various objects to pour, scoop, measure, dump, retrieve objects, splash, wash, and generally handle water in as many ways as possible.

ADAPTATIONS:

■ Vary the motor task to change the skill. For example, picking up poker chips from under water is a fine motor task; pouring from a large bucket into a small cup is a large motor task.

■ Alter the temperature of the water by adding ice cubes.

■ Vary the texture of items used. A soft cloth feels different from a sponge with a scrubbing surface on the back.

■ Add intensity to the task when washing and scrubbing.

INNOVATOR:

Sue Grosse
Milwaukee High School of the Arts

GAME:	CATEGORY:
CLEAN UP YOUR ROOM!	**AQUATICS**

GOAL:

To improve water orientation, group cooperation, balance, agility, and CR endurance.

OBJECTIVE:

Students move around the playing area, locate a ball, and push it toward the opponent's area, continuing the activity for 3 minutes.

EQUIPMENT:

Two lane lines and twice as many small floating balls as there are people.

SETUP:

Put lane lines in a "T" formation in the pool with at least 10 balls on each part of the "T."

DESCRIPTION:

In shallow water (up to chest deep) secure one lane line widthwise and another lengthwise (see illustration). Next, place equal numbers of students in each rectangle, marked 1 and 2. Then place double the number of balls as students in each playing area. On a signal, students begin to push the balls to the other side. The objective of the game is to have no balls on your side of the pool when the game is stopped. No throwing; balls must be pushed only. Students move constantly to locate and push balls to the opposite side of the lane line. Suggested time limit is 3 minutes. When play is completed, count how many balls are left on each side, or play the game just for fun.

ADAPTATIONS:

■ Use very bright balls for students who are partially sighted.

■ Use flotation devices, such as a buoyancy belt or a life jacket, for students with limited mobility.

● Balls   Team 1

Lane lines

Team 2

■ Larger balls, balloons, or Ping-Pong balls can also be used (however, Ping-Pong balls may get sucked into the gutter of some pools).

■ A sound device can be placed behind one playing area for orientation.

■ Helpers can be in the water to orient individuals who have multiple disabilities.

■ Helpers can be placed at lane lines to return stray balls and players.

INNOVATOR:
Monica Lepore
West Chester University

GAME:	CATEGORY:
CLOTHES SWIM	**AQUATICS (ALL AGES)**

GOAL:
To improve CR and muscular endurance and increase water adjustment and safety by being prepared for accidental submersion wearing clothes.

OBJECTIVE:
Students participate in water activities wearing clothes.

EQUIPMENT:

Long-sleeved shirts, long pants, old tennis shoes (all clean).

SETUP:

Pool with depth appropriate to swimming ability.

DESCRIPTION:

Participants wear clothes over their swimsuits. Students enter the pool and perform usual pool activities wearing their clothes. The class members discuss what is different about being in the pool with clothes on, how it feels, what might happen in an accident situation, and how they can help themselves.

ADAPTATIONS:

■ Expand the activity to include disrobing.

■ Expand the activity to include clothing flotation.

■ Expand the activity to include using personal flotation devices such as life jackets or buoyancy belts.

INNOVATOR:

Sue Grosse
Milwaukee High School of the Arts

GAME:	CATEGORY:
DUCK **SWIM**	**AQUATICS** **(ALL AGES)**

GOAL:

To improve arm and leg strength, stroke pattern, CR and muscular endurance, and flexibility.

OBJECTIVE:

Students practice arm and hand position and/or leg position during stroking action. Improved positioning will result in increased muscle strength and more efficient stroke.

EQUIPMENT:

Swim Fins and Wave Webs (hand mitts with webbing between the fingers made by Hydro Fit, 440 Charnelton, Eugene, OR 97401).

SETUP:

Pool with depth appropriate to swimming ability.

DESCRIPTION:

Students perform the arm stroke pattern and/or leg kick pattern wearing mitts and/or fins (use either mitts or fins—not both at the same time—until individuals get used to them). Fins are particularly useful for crawl stroke kicks. Mitts can be used for any arm pattern.

ADAPTATIONS:

■ Vary the size of the fins. Stiffer, larger fins require more leg strength. Smaller, more flexible fins require less leg strength.

■ Vary the hand position once mitts are on. Fingers together is the desired form (end result). Having fingers spread uses the web action of the mitt (which helps participants learn the reason for cupped hands and builds arm strength).

INNOVATOR:

Sue Grosse
Milwaukee High School of the Arts

GAME:	CATEGORY:
FIND THE DUCKY	**AQUATICS (ELEMENTARY)**

GOAL:

To improve water adjustment, auditory focusing in the pool, spatial orientation, and cardiorespiratory endurance.

OBJECTIVE:

Students locate and move to touch a squeaky toy.

EQUIPMENT:

Plastic duck or other floatable identified toy that makes a noise.

SETUP:

In the pool, rope off a shallow area.

DESCRIPTION:

Within a contained shallow area, individuals move to locate and touch a toy they hear squeaking or making a noise. The toy is activated by the teacher, aide, or other students.

ADAPTATIONS:

■ Use several different toys with different sounds. Put them in a variety of locations. Individuals must locate a specific toy with a specific noise.

■ Individuals must perform a specific locomotor movement to get to the noise.

■ Students may perform the activity with partners.

■ Students who are deaf-blind or with physical disabilities may need help to understand the game, locate the ball, and so on.

INNOVATOR:
Sue Grosse
Milwaukee High School of the Arts

GAME:	CATEGORY:
FLOWER HUNT	**AQUATICS**

GOAL:
To improve underwater swimming, breath control, search and find technique, and cardiorespiratory endurance.

OBJECTIVE:
Students swim under water, locate an object, then surface.

EQUIPMENT:
Plastic flowers, each flower containing enough washers to make it sink. Use two to three times as many flowers as there are students, depending upon their ability.

SETUP:
Place the plastic flowers in a straight line across the bottom of the shallow end of the pool.

DESCRIPTION:
Swimmers (three or four at a time) submerge at the wall and probe the bottom of the pool with their hands to grab the flowers. They must swim with the flowers to the other side and show the teacher what they have found. Then the students drop the flowers to the bottom of the pool for the next group.

ADAPTATIONS:
■ Let students walk until they feel the flowers and then bob down to get them.

■ Allow beginner swimmers to retrieve flowers with their feet.

■ Students with limited ability can retrieve floating flowers or flowers placed in close proximity.

Adapted from American Red Cross Film "Focus on Ability."

INNOVATOR:

Contributed by Monica Lepore
West Chester University

GAME:	CATEGORY:
LAP COUNTING	**AQUATICS**

GOAL:

To improve cardiorespiratory endurance, muscular endurance and strength, and independence in swimming laps.

OBJECTIVE:

Students swim laps independently and count on their own. (Note: Many students who are good swimmers do not swim independently because they are prompt-dependent—that is, they depend on a staff person to tell them to continue each time they reach the end of the pool. Some students will wait at one end of the pool throughout the class period if someone does not tell them to keep going or swim more laps. This behavior is usually associated with autism, Rubella, or mental retardation. This activity will help decrease or eliminate prompts and aid students in becoming independent swimmers.

EQUIPMENT:

Large plastic containers (crates, for example) and diving rings or sticks.

SETUP:

Place rings or sticks at one end of the pool, and the plastic containers at the other. (Place a challenging number of rings or sticks on the deck—e.g., if students can normally swim 10 laps, give them 11 or 12 rings or sticks.)

DESCRIPTION:

Students start swimming from the end of the pool that has the plastic containers. They swim a length, pick up a ring or stick, and swim back to the container. The rings or sticks are placed in the container. Students

continue swimming until all rings or sticks have been placed in the container.

ADAPTATIONS:

■ Use objects that are reinforcing to your students.

■ Students can swim laps for time.

■ Students with limited ability can swim widths of the pool.

■ Students who are blind or deaf-blind can utilize the lane markers and sides of the pool as directional prompts.

■ If students have a hard time performing their stroke while holding the ring or stick, try the following: Create an easy way to carry the object, change the object, use flip cards with numbers to indicate completed laps, or place the plastic containers and diving rings or sticks at the same end of the pool.

INNOVATOR:

Monica Kleeman
Perkins School for the Blind

GAME:	CATEGORY:
LEADER IN THE CIRCLE	**AQUATICS**

GOAL:
To improve pre-swimming skills.

OBJECTIVE:
Students take turns leading the class in performing various pre-swimming skills.

EQUIPMENT:
One ball.

SETUP:
Students get into a circle formation.

DESCRIPTION:
Students pass the ball around the circle, singing: "Round and round the circle we go, where it stops nobody knows, 1-2-3-4-5!" When they reach "5" the student with the ball tells the rest of the class which pre-swimming skill to perform as well as the number of repetitions or a time limit—for example, float on your back for 15 seconds, jump up and down 10 times, submerge for 5 seconds, etc.

ADAPTATIONS:
■ Students with limited ability may need a flotation device or physical assistance.

■ Students can perform the skills with partners.

■ Challenge the better swimmers with more repetitions or more difficult skills.

■ Students who are deaf or deaf-blind may need a volunteer, a teacher, or an interpreter to aid in communication.

■ Students with limited mobility may push the ball to pass it around the circle.

INNOVATOR:
Monica Kleeman
Perkins School for the Blind

GAME:	CATEGORY:
MUSICAL HOOPS	**AQUATICS**

GOAL:

To learn to start and stop to music, personal space location, breath control, and to improve CR and muscular endurance.

OBJECTIVE:

Swimmers move clockwise around a shallow area in a predetermined movement, duck under a hoop when the music stops, and perform an aquatic skill in the hoop.

EQUIPMENT:

Hoops and music.

SETUP:

In the pool, the same number of hoops as there are participants are spread through shallow water (or deep water if students are good swimmers).

DESCRIPTION:

To start the game, a helper on the deck puts on music, and all students run, skip, hop, swim (beginner stroke, breaststroke, etc.), or the like in one direction (e.g., clockwise). When the music stops, all participants must feel for a hoop, duck under and into it, and perform a designated skill, such as bob three times, prone floating for 5 seconds (whatever challenges each player). When the music begins again, they resume circling until the music stops again.

ADAPTATIONS:

■ For more challenges, vary the locomotor movement or swimming stroke.

■ For nonswimmers stress bobbing, blowing bubbles, and so forth in the hoop.

■ Individuals who are more physically disabled can move in a tube; when the music stops, they locate a hoop and place it over their head and execute a designated skill—for example, move with the assistance of a volunteer, perform a locomotor or swimming movement within their ability, etc.

■ Take away one hoop, allowing two students to share a hoop when the music stops.

Data from American Red Cross, 1977, *Adapted acquatics* (Garden City, N.Y.: Doubleday).

INNOVATOR:

Contributed by Monica Lepore
West Chester University

GAME:	CATEGORY:
POOL ACTIVITIES	**AQUATICS (ELEMENTARY)**

GOAL:

To improve water adjustment skills, agility, balance, CR and muscular endurance, and fundamental motor patterns and skills.

OBJECTIVE:

Students walk, jump, skip, run, hop, or gallop the width of the pool in chest-deep water.

SETUP:

Swimming pool shallow enough for the students to stand comfortably in chest-deep water.

DESCRIPTION:

Students enter the pool in chest-deep water. The teacher tells the student the locomotor skill to use while crossing the pool. The student performs the skill. If the student has difficulty with the skill, the teacher may manually manipulate the student or model the skill to reinforce the motion. Once the student has performed the chosen skill, he or she may have an easier time transferring it to land. If the skill is performed in the pool, yet is difficult on land, the student needs to continue working on the skill in the pool until he or she can successfully perform the skill on land. Students may work in partners for help with balance and cooperation.

ADAPTATIONS:

■ When students have mastered a skill, have relay races of either one width or two of the chosen skill.

■ If a student is having a hard time with one skill, break down the skill, teach each sub-skill separately, and then integrate the separate sub-skills into the desired skill.

■ See how many times students can cross the pool using a different skill each time. Can they add a new skill to their repertoire?

■ Play follow the leader in the shallow end, with different skills and different leaders. Suggested commands include: "Can you do it backwards?" "Hop as high as you can!" and "Swing your arms forward!"

■ Students with low or no vision may need an auditory cue to the side of the pool, especially if they are afraid.

INNOVATOR:

Lauren Lieberman
SUNY Brockport

GAME:	CATEGORY:
POOL PARACHUTE	**AQUATICS**

GOAL:

To improve group cooperation, water adjustment, swimming skills, flexibility, CR endurance, and muscular strength.

OBJECTIVE:

Students cooperatively play parachute activities.

EQUIPMENT:

6-foot parachute.

SETUP:

No setup is required.

DESCRIPTION:

Students hold onto the parachute in a circle in the shallow end of the pool. They then walk in circles to the left or right. On the count of three they pull the parachute under the water and stretch it tightly so that no part of it is near the surface. At this point, the teacher calls a student's name, and that student swims over the parachute to the other side.

ADAPTATIONS:

■ Students who cannot stand in the shallow end should wear a flotation device for the game.

■ Students who need help standing may be provided assistance by a volunteer, or may stand against a wall for support.

■ Use sponge balls to bounce on the parachute.

■ Students who are blind or deaf-blind should be given descriptions of what is happening with the parachute to increase levels of excitement.

■ Students with limited mobility may hold onto the parachute and float around the circle.

■ Without lifting the parachute, have students and staff pull the parachute tight. Then the students can sit on top of the parachute while it is being moved around in a circle.

INNOVATOR:
Monica Kleeman
Perkins School for the Blind

GAME:	CATEGORY:
■ **SCAVENGER HUNT**	**AQUATICS (ALL AGES)**

GOAL:
To learn submersion and underwater swimming, improve cardiovascular endurance, flexibility, and muscular strength.

OBJECTIVE:
Students submerge, search for, and retrieve specific items.

EQUIPMENT:
A variety of sinkable objects: cap, dive ring, cup, wash cloth, spoon, lock, and so on, and a scavenger hunt list (written on chalkboard, brailled on laminated paper, or pictures of objects).

SETUP:

Pool with depth level appropriate to the swimming ability of participants.

DESCRIPTION:

Individuals are divided into two teams. Each team is given a different list of equipment that has been sunken across the whole swimming area (lists can be read to participants). Participants must find items on their lists.

ADAPTATIONS:

■ Vary the length of the list.

■ Vary the size of items (be sure small items won't go down drains).

■ If students are at very different ability levels, make a rule that each student must collect a certain number of items. Allow students to work in pairs if necessary.

■ Students who are deaf or deaf-blind will need to have directions signed to them.

■ Include objects that buzz, jingle, ring, etc. where possible for students who are blind. The students may also be buddied up with a peer.

■ For students with physical disabilities, volunteers or peers may provide assistance as needed in retrieving objects.

INNOVATOR:

Sue Grosse
Milwaukee High School of the Arts

GAME:	CATEGORY:
SPONGE PARTNERS	**AQUATICS**

GOAL:

To improve water adjustment skills, cooperation, and socialization.

OBJECTIVE:

Students take a sponge with a specific shape and find a partner who has the same sponge.

EQUIPMENT:

One sponge for each student (two of each kind of sponge—e.g., two round sponges, two square, two large, two small).

SETUP:
   Students stand in a circle in the shallow end of the pool.

DESCRIPTION:
   Students put their hands behind their backs, and the instructor places a
   sponge in each person's hands. On "Go" the students feel the shape of
   their sponges, then move around the pool and try to find the student who
   has the same shaped sponge. They cannot talk, but they can bring their
   sponges out from behind their backs. When a student finds his or her
   partner, they move as fast as they can together to the wall. The goal is
   to be the first pair to find their sponge partner and reach the wall.

ADAPTATIONS:
   ■ Add a challenge by having all students keep the sponges behind
   their backs for the entire game.

   ■ Instead of sponges, use objects of different textures.

   ■ Students who cannot move independently in the shallow end can
   wear a flotation device or receive assistance from an aide or volunteer.

■ In addition to using the sense of touch to locate similar objects, students can use their voices to describe the object.

■ Students who are deaf or deaf-blind will need to communicate using sign language.

■ Once students find a partner with a sponge of the same shape or color, they may participate in "body painting."

INNOVATOR:

Monica Kleeman

Perkins School for the Blind

GAME:

THE WEATHER GAME

CATEGORY:

AQUATICS

GOAL:

To improve water orientation, breath control, distinguishing weather, socialization, listening, and following directions.

OBJECTIVE:

Students follow commands to perform various skills in an aquatics setting.

EQUIPMENT:

None.

SETUP:

Students are spread out in the shallow end of the pool either in a circle or scattered so there is enough space between them to move freely.

DESCRIPTION:

Either the teacher or one of the students is the "weatherperson," who gives students the following commands to perform:

- Sunshine—place both arms overhead resembling a circle.

- Rain—splash water up with your hands.

- Tornado—place arms out to the side splashing, and spin your body in a circle.

- Thunder—go underwater and blow large bubbles, making sounds like thunder.

- Snow—splash quietly and gently.

- Windy—put face in the water and blow bubbles.

ADAPTATIONS:

- Students may make up their own weather conditions.

- Students who are deaf-blind will need someone to explain the game, communicate commands, and so forth.

- Let students use their imagination when acting out weather.

- Change the "weatherperson" frequently.

- Provide assistance to students having difficulty demonstrating movements.

- Use signs to communicate with students who are deaf or deaf-blind.

INNOVATOR:

Linda Webbert
Maryland School for the Blind

GAME:	CATEGORY:
UNDERWATER TAG	**AQUATICS (ALL AGES)**

GOAL:

To improve submersion adjustment, breath control, swimming skill, speed, and cardiovascular and muscular endurance.

OBJECTIVE:

Students voluntarily submerge completely, holding their breath and blowing bubbles.

EQUIPMENT:

None.

SETUP:

Pool with depth level appropriate to swimming ability of participants.

DESCRIPTION:

One person is "it." All others try to avoid being tagged by "it" and thus becoming "it" by ducking under water when "it" comes close to them. A person cannot be tagged by "it" if he or she ducks underwater before being tagged.

ADAPTATIONS:

■ A player who ducks underwater but comes right back up can be tagged. "It" counts to five, and if the person does not come up, "it" must move on to try to catch another.

■ Make the bottom of the pool "safe." Participants who are touching the bottom with a hand cannot be tagged.

■ Change the rules for students who have limited breath control abilities—for example, submerge to mouth, nose, or eyes.

■ "It" can ring a bell to alert other players of his or her location. In turn, the others can be required to regularly call "it's" name in order to keep "it" aware of their locations.

INNOVATOR:

Sue Grosse
Milwaukee High School of the Arts

GAME:	CATEGORY:
WATER BASEBALL	**AQUATICS**

GOAL:

To improve the sidearm strike, water running, underwater swimming, game skills, and muscular and CR endurance.

OBJECTIVE:

A student on offense (batter) sidearm strikes a ball and swims underwater to a predetermined spot before returning to home base. At the same time, a student on defense locates the ball and tries to swim with it to home base and back to the defensive wall before the batter reaches home.

EQUIPMENT:
One or two cones, a beach ball containing bells, and two spoons.

SETUP:
The following diagram shows the setup:

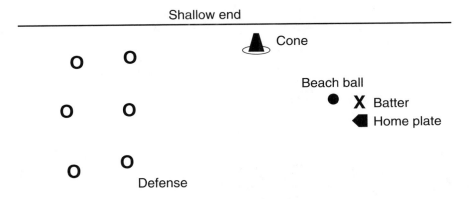

DESCRIPTION:
One player strikes a beach ball containing bells from one side of the pool to the other, where the defense waits. The striker then swims underwater to the other side (or to a cone under water where a guide is striking two spoons together) and then back home. The defense player who retrieves the ball swims with it to home plate and then back to the defensive wall. If the base runner gets back to home plate before the defender reaches the defensive wall, he or she earns a point for his or her team. Rotate defensive positioning if one player dominates, or make a rule that a defensive player cannot touch the ball twice in a row. Members of the defensive team should help with orientation by calling their teammate's name. A helper with spoons should orient the base runner (i.e., hitter) toward home plate. Each member of the offense gets a turn before switching sides.

ADAPTATIONS:
■ Nonswimmers can run, or paddle with a flotation device, to the sound of spoons or clapping.

■ Individuals with multiple disabilities may use helpers for guidance or for support on offense and defense.

■ In order to include all defensive players, change the rules so that, rather than a single defensive player having to swim across the pool and back, the ball must be passed around the entire defense team; each person receiving the ball must perform a predetermined task (e.g., jump five times, bob three times, float on his or her back for 5 seconds) before passing it on to the next person. The last player to receive the ball gives it back to the player who originally got the ball from offense, and the ball is considered to be home at that point.

■ To keep interest high, have a sighted announcer give play-by-play descriptions of the game for all the students.

INNOVATOR:
Monica Lepore
West Chester University

GAME:	CATEGORY:
WATER SOCCER	**AQUATICS**

GOAL:

To improve kicking skills, arm strokes, teamwork, and muscular and CR endurance.

OBJECTIVE:

Students kick a ball hard enough to make the ball pass the other team's line of players and score. All students may participate in this game.

EQUIPMENT:

A playground ball or beach ball.

SETUP:

Students form two lines in the pool facing each other 8-10 feet apart. The ball is placed in the center of the two lines. The line formation may be in the shallow or deep end depending upon the skill level, endurance, and confidence of the students.

DESCRIPTION:

Students float prone or supine. On the signal "Go" the students kick as hard as they can and try to make the ball go past the other team. One point is scored each time the ball passes the other team. Where necessary students may use a flotation device or physical assistance for the game.

ADAPTATIONS:

▪ The same game can be played on land in the gym. The ball must stay on the ground, and points can be scored in the same manner. This has proven to be a big hit with elementary students!

▪ The same game may be played prone using arm strokes.

▪ The game can be played one on one.

▪ The instructor may describe the position of the ball to increase awareness and excitement for students who are blind.

▪ The instructor may use more than one ball.

INNOVATOR:

Lauren Lieberman
SUNY Brockport

REFERENCES AND SELECTED RESOURCES

American Red Cross. (1974). "Focus on Ability." Produced by John S. Allen. Audio-Visual Production Center. Videocassette.

American Red Cross. (1977). *Adapted Aquatics: Swimming for Persons with Physical or Mental Impairments.* Garden City, NY: Doubleday.

Anderson, L. (1989). *U.S. Swimming Handbook for Adapted Competitive Swimming.* Colorado Springs: U.S.A. Swimming.

Anderson, W. (1968). *Teaching the Physically Handicapped to Swim.* London: Faber and Faber.

Association of Swimming Therapy. (1992). *Swimming for People with Disabilities.* London: A. & C. Black.

Bull, E., Holderson, J., Kahrs, N., Mathiesen, G., Mogensen, I., Torheim, A., and Uldal, M. (1985). *In the Pool: Swimming Instruction for the Disabled.* Reston, VA: AAHPERD.

Campion, M. (1986). *Hydrotherapy in Pediatrics.* Rockville, MD: Aspen Systems.

Cowart, J. (1993). "Adapted Instructional and Equipment Ideas for Use with Students Who Are Multiply Handicapped Blind Within a Leisure Time Context." In Jansma, P. (ed.), *The Psychomotor Domain Training and Serious Disabilities* (4th edition). New York: University Press of America.

Frontiera, D. (1986). *It's OK to be Afraid of the Water.* Byron, CA: Front Row Experience.

Graham, G., Holt, Hale, S.A., and Parker, M. (1980). *Children Moving: A Teacher's Guide to Developing a Successful Physical Education Program.* Mountain View, CA: Mayfield.

Harrison, J. (ed.). (1989). *Anyone Can Swim.* Marlborough, Wiltshire, England: The Crowood Press.

Hyman, D. (1969). "Teaching the Blind Student Archery Skills." *Journal for Health, Physical Education and Recreation*, **40**, 85-86.

Marsallo, M., and Vacante, D. (1983). *Adapted Games and Motor Activities for Children.* Annandale, VA: Marsallo/Vacante.

McClenaghan, B., and Gallahue, D. (1978). *Fundamental Movement: A Developmental and Remedial Approach.* Philadelphia: W.B. Saunders.

Reams, D. (1980). *Archery Project Com PAC.* Miami: Dade County Public Schools.

Special Olympics Swimming and Diving. (Available from Special Olympics International, 1350 New York Ave., N.W., Ste. 500, Washington, DC 20006)

Taylor, T. (1953). "The Unseen Target." *Journal of Health, Physical Education and Recreation*, **24**, 15 and 51.

Thomas, D. (1989). *Swimming: Steps to Success.* Champaign, IL: Leisure Press.

White, E. (1995). "Making Archery a Sport for the Visually Impaired." *Strategies*, **8**, 12-14.

YMCA Progressive Swimming Instructor's Guide. (1986). Champaign, IL: Human Kinetics.

YMCA of the USA. (1987). *Aquatics for Special Populations.* Champaign, IL: YMCA Program Store.

Appendix A

Classifications of Blindness and Deafness

Students who are labeled blind, deaf, hard of hearing, visually impaired, and so forth all have a wide range of sensory abilities. In order to determine the appropriate adaptations and teaching strategies it is important to know the amount of hearing and vision a student possesses. The following two charts will aid in understanding the labels in a student's file.

Classifications of Blindness

Visual handicaps are defined in terms of visual acuity as measured by a Snellen chart. The lines of progressively smaller letters are read by a person sitting or standing at a distance of 20 feet from the chart. Sharpness or clearness of vision is designated as a numerical ratio. One of the following classifications may appear on a student's school record:

20/200—*legal blindness.* The ability to see at 20 feet what the normal eye can see at 200 feet. This classification makes the student eligible to receive assistance under state and federal programs.

5/200 to 10/200—*travel vision.* The ability to see at 5 to 10 feet what persons with normal vision see at 200 feet.

3/200 to 5/200—*motion perception.* The ability to see at 3 to 5 feet what persons with normal vision see at 200 feet. This ability is limited almost entirely to motion.

Less than 3/200—*light perception.* The ability to distinguish a strong light at a distance of 3 feet from the eye, but inability to detect movement of a hand at the same distance.

Lack of visual perception—*total blindness.* This is the inability to recognize a strong light that is shown directly into the eye.

Classifications of Deafness

Degree of Loss	Loss in Decibels	Difficulty with
Slight	25-40	Whispered speech
Mild	41-54	Normal speech at a distance greater than 3-5 feet
Marked or moderate	55-69	Understanding loud or shouted speech at close range; group discussion
Severe	70-89	Understanding speech at a close range, even when amplified
Profound	90+	Hearing most sounds, including telephone rings and musical instruments

Appendix B

Tips for Teaching Students Who Are Visually Impaired

1. **Treat the child as part of the class.** The same disciplinary rules should apply to everyone. Make exceptions only when necessary, just as you would for any other child.

2. **Speak naturally when you talk.** Don't be afraid to use words that refer to seeing. However, the words "here" and "there" are too general for descriptive use. Be specific, and label objects that give direction and location.

3. **Gestures are not always enough.** In a group setting, call the child by name when you want a response from them.

4. **Use sound to help the child.** Your voice leads and directs a visually impaired child within the environment. Get the child's attention before giving instructions. A moving speaker confuses a child. Describe with clear directions and in a normal speaking voice where you are and how the child can reach you.

5. **Help make the sound environment meaningful for the visually impaired child.** Eliminate confusing or conflicting sounds. The sorting of sounds is a difficult skill which takes time, experience, and explanation to develop.

6. **Explain what is happening around the child.** Show where sounds and smells are coming from. As the child explores, describe everything with variety, quality, and richness.

7. **Orient the child to the classroom and equipment in the gym.** Let the child know if you have changed the room around. Independent mobility is important and sometimes difficult for visually impaired children.

8. **Avoid overprotection.** Remember that all children get bumps and scrapes occasionally. Safety is important, but overprotection can be just as detrimental to a child as underprotection.

9. **Encourage independence.** Let the children do as much as possible for themselves.

10. **Build the child's self-confidence by letting them try.** Take the child through an activity or game a couple of times before requiring independent movement. For a sighted child, motor imitation is a visual skill,

whereas a visually impaired child needs to experience the activity physically.

11. **Answer questions simply and naturally.** The other children will ask questions about a visually impaired child.

12. **Consider the available light sources.** Light can be distracting for some partially sighted children, while for others indirect lighting may be inadequate.

13. **Teach the child through the remaining senses.** A visually impaired child cannot learn by observing and imitating the action of others. You may need to physically put the child through an action or allow the child to experience the actions you are performing.

14. **State your name when approaching a visually impaired child.** Voices are not always easy to identify, particularly in crowds or stress situations. Also, introduce others in the room, especially if they are newcomers or people who are not usually in the classroom.

15. **Relay accurate information to the visually impaired child in order to maintain a sense of trust.**

16. **Address the student directly, not through a companion or guide.**

17. **If you are talking to a blind student and you have to leave, tell him or her that you are leaving!** People look silly talking to themselves thinking you are there.

18. **Do not raise your voice or shout so the blind person will understand you better, unless the person is hearing-impaired also.**

19. **Doors should be completely closed or completely open.** A half-open door is a hazard to a blind person.

20. **Do not be a servant.** Do things together.

21. **Ropes taped to the floor help visually impaired students to identify activity boundaries.**

22. **Occasionally blindfold the sighted students and play a game.** This increases empathy for and acceptance of the blind student.

23. **Do not think of them as blind children.** They are children who happen to be blind.

Appendix C

Resources for Recreation and Sport

American Alliance for Health, Physical Education, Recreation and Dance

    1900 Association Drive
    Reston, VA 22091
    703-476-3400 Fax: 703-476-9527

Students, educators in physical education, health, recreation and dance. Houses the Adapted Physical Activity Council. Operates Information and Resource Utilization Center devoted to physical education and recreation for individuals with disabilities.

American Athletic Association for the Deaf

    3607 Washington Boulevard, #4
    Ogden, UT 84403-1737
    801-393-7916 Fax: 801-393-2263

Fosters athletic competition among deaf people and regulates uniform rules governing such competition. Regional, state, and local groups.

Association for the Education of the Visually Handicapped— Bulletin for Physical Educators

    919 Walnut Street
    Philadelphia, PA 19103

Blind Outdoor Leisure Development

    533 East Main Street
    Aspen, CO 81611
    303-925-2086

Assists individuals who are blind in participating in outdoor recreation. Aids in the establishment of local recreation clubs. Designs and conducts training courses.

Braille Sports Foundation

    730 Hennepin Avenue, Room 301
    Minneapolis, MN 55402

Colorado Outdoor Center for the Handicapped

    P.O. Box 697
    Breckenridge, CO 80424

Feeling Sports Magazine

    4601 Excelsior Avenue South
    St. Louis Park, MN 55416

National Beep Baseball Association

    Jeanette Bigger
    2231 West 1st Avenue
    Topeka, KS 66606-1304
    913-276-0345 913-234-2156

National Handicapped Sports

    451 Hungerford Drive, Suite 100
    Rockville, MD 20850
    800-966-4647
    Fax: 301-217-0968
          301-217-0960

Promotes sports and recreation opportunities for individuals with physical disabilities. Provides direct services to people with mobility impairments, including those with visual impairments, head injuries, cerebral palsy, birth defects, and neuromuscular disabilities.

Ski for Light Inc.

    1455 West Lake Street
    Minneapolis, MN 55408

United States Association for Blind Athletes (USABA)

    33 North Institute Street
    Colorado Springs, CO 80903
    719-630-0422 Fax: 719-578-4654

Aims to develop individual independence through athletic competition.

United States Cerebral Palsy Athletic Association
  34578 Warren Road, Suite 264
  Westland, MI 48184

U.S. Toy Library Association
  2530 Crawford Avenue
  Evanston, IL 60201-4954
  National network of nearly 400 toy lending libraries serving children with and without disabilities. Seeks to broaden understanding of how toys can educate and aid in development and therapy of children with disabilities. Families may borrow both commercially available and adapted toys.

Wheelchair Sports Foundation
  c/o Benjamin H. Lipton
  40-24 62nd Street
  Woodside, NY 11377

World Recreation Association of the Deaf, Inc. USA
  P.O. Box 92074
  Rochester, NY 14692-0074
  TTY: 716-586-4208
  Fax: 716-475-7101
  Established to foster the development of innovation in recreation and cultural activities for the deaf and hard-of-hearing community.

In addition to this list there are many other sources for recreation and sport for individuals who are sensory-impaired. In most cities you will find a Light House for the Blind, a Deaf Club, a Federation for the Blind, an Association for the Blind, a Deaf/Blind contact center, and Associations for the Deaf. These are places to contact that may help you find other resources.

Taken in part from:

Deaf-Blind Link Fact Sheet Insert:
  800-854-7013 TTY
  800-438-9376 Voice

Jones, J.(1988). *Training Guide to Cerebral Palsy Sports.* Champaign, IL: Human Kinetics.

Rural Special Education Quarterly. Spring 1990,Vol. 10, No. 3, 65-66.

Winnick, J.P. (1990). *Adapted Physical Education and Sport.* Champaign, IL: Human Kinetics, 466-468.

Appendix D

Equipment Resource List

American Federation for the Blind
Goal Ball equipment
1-800-AFBLIND

Canadian Blind Sports Association
Showdown (rules and equipment)
333 River Road
Ottowa, ON KIL 8H9
Canada

Flaghouse
Minibeeper
Adapted bowling ball
Therapeutic equipment
150 North MacQuesten Parkway
Mt. Vernon, NY 10550

Gym Closet
Horseshoes
Sports equipment for all abilities

Hydro Fit
Swim Fins
Wave Webs
440 Charnelton
Eugene, OR 97401

National Beep Baseball Association
Beep Baseball equipment
2231 West First Street
Topeka, KS 66606

Pro Optics
Blindfolds
317 Woodwork Lane
Palatine, IL 60057

Sportime/Abilitations (Catalogue for Therapy and Rehabilitation)
Goal Balls
Parachute
Balzac balls
Ball on string (kick, throw, bat)
Various sensory stimulating equipment
One Sportime Way
Atlanta, GA 30340

Wham-O, Inc.
Frisbees
Sports Promotion Department
835 East El Monte Street
San Gabriel, CA 91778

York Archery Supply
Archery equipment
P.O. Box 110
Independence, MO 64051

About the Authors

Lauren J. Lieberman is a faculty member in the Department of Physical Education and Sport at the State University of New York at Brockport. She earned a PhD in 1995 in human performance with a minor in movement studies and disabilities from Oregon State University where she also taught classes in adapted physical education and coordinated a play-based program for infants and toddlers.

From 1989 to 1993 Lieberman was an instructor in adapted physical education and aquatics and taught in the deaf-blind program at the Perkins School for the Blind in Watertown, Massachusetts. In addition, she coached students with multiple sensory impairments and was a consultant for the Perkins School's Severely Impaired Program.

Since 1987 Lieberman, who holds a teaching certificate in health and physical education for grades K-12, also has coordinated many programs in physical education and recreation for individuals with sensory impairments. She frequently gives presentations and workshops, and she is a consultant for a project to establish national standards for adapted physical education specialists.

James F. Cowart is an adapted physical education teacher at the California School for the Blind in Fremont, California. He received an MA in education from the University of San Francisco. A veteran teacher of adapted physical education, Cowart has won numerous awards, most recently the 1996 Adapted Physical Activity Council National Adapted Physical Education Teacher of the Year Award, given by the American Alliance for Health, Physical Education, Recreation and Dance. Cowart's writings on the subject of adapted physical education have been published widely.